COST–BENEFIT ANALYSIS

A Handbook

OPERATIONS RESEARCH
AND INDUSTRIAL ENGINEERING

Consulting Editor: J. William Schmidt

CBM, Inc., Cleveland, Ohio

Applied Statistical Methods, *I. W. Burr*

Mathematical Foundations of Management Science and Systems Analysis, *J. William Schmidt*

Urban Systems Models, *Walter Helly*

Introduction to Discrete Linear Controls: Theory and Application, *Albert B. Bishop*

Integer Programming: Theory, Applications, and Computations, *Hamdy A. Taha*

Transform Techniques for Probability Modeling, *Walter C. Giffin*

Analysis of Queueing Systems, *J. A. White, J. W. Schmidt, and G. K. Bennett*

Models for Public Systems Analysis, *Edward J. Beltrami*

Computer Methods in Operations Research, *Arne Thesen*

Cost-Benefit Analysis: A Handbook, *Peter G. Sassone and William A. Schaffer*

Modeling of Complex Systems, *V. Vemuri*

Applied Linear Programming: For The Socioeconomic and Environmental Sciences, *Michael Greenberg*

COST-BENEFIT
ANALYSIS
A Handbook

Peter G. Sassone *and* William A. Schaffer
COLLEGE OF INDUSTRIAL MANAGEMENT
GEORGIA INSTITUTE OF TECHNOLOGY
ATLANTA, GEORGIA

ACADEMIC PRESS   New York   San Francisco   London   1978
A SUBSIDIARY OF HARCOURT BRACE JOVANOVICH, PUBLISHERS

ACADEMIC PRESS, INC.
111 Fifth Avenue, New York, New York 10003

United Kingdom Edition published by
ACADEMIC PRESS, INC. (LONDON) LTD.
24/28 Oval Road, London NW1   7DX

Library of Congress Cataloging in Publication Data

Sassone, Peter G.
    Cost-benefit analysis.

    (Operations research and industrial engineering series)
    Bibliography: p.
    Includes index.
    1.   Cost effectiveness.   I.   Schaffer, William A.,
joint author.   II.   Title.
HD47.S318   658.1'552   77-6612
ISBN 0-12-619350-9

To

CHARLOTTE and LEE

CONTENTS

9   **Performing a Cost–Benefit Analysis**

Bibliography

PREFACE

This book attempts to bridge a gap in the literature of project appraisal, or cost–benefit analysis (CBA). Several fine theoretical treatments of CBA exist, including works by Mishan, Dasgupta and Pierce, Eckstein, and McKean. Professional economists, including ourselves, have benefited greatly from the efforts of these authors. By and large, these books are addressed to economists and treat their material solely on a topic-by-topic basis. This book is addressed to practicing cost–benefit analysts (who may not be graduate economists), to government officials who commission, oversee, and use cost–benefit studies, to citizens who wish to understand the workings of an analysis that may recommend turning their favorite trout stream into a lake, and to students in such courses as environmental economics, engineering economics, applied microeconomics, applied welfare economics, public sector decision making, and, of course, cost–benefit analysis.

We have attempted to present not only a lucid explanation of topics, but a synthesis of these topics into an overall design for carrying out a cost–benefit analysis. Throughout, the material is accessible to readers with little or no formal training in economics. However, we have not hesitated to use basic algebra and geometry as expository tools, and a small amount of elementary calculus is found interspersed throughout the text. Readers familiar with calculus will find that its use simplifies the understanding of economic concepts; those unfamiliar with it should have no difficulty with the concepts as presented in the text alone.

ACKNOWLEDGMENTS

This work began with a research project, carried out by the Engineering Experiment Station at the Georgia Institute of Technology and entitled, Cost-Benefit Methodology with Example Application to the Use of Wind Generators. Sponsored by the Lewis Research Center of the National Aeronautics and Space Administration (NASA), the project involved developing and documenting cost-benefit methods usable by NASA personnel (primarily engineers). The NASA project monitor was Dr. Gerry Hein, and the Georgia Tech project director was Robert P. Zimmer, now chief of the Systems Engineering Division of the Engineering Experiment Station. We are indebted to both men for their many helpful comments and especially for their insistence that our exposition of concepts be as concrete as possible. Since the initial development of the manuscript in 1974, the procedures have been tested and refined through application to a number of cost-benefit projects. Among these are Cost-Benefits of Space Communication Technologies (NASA Lewis Research Center), The Climatic Impact Assessment Program (U.S. Department of Transportation), A Cost-Benefit Analysis of Information Analysis Centers (National Science Foundation), Assessment of Wind Energy for Northeast Utilities (Energy Research and Development Administration), Benefit Assessment of Pollution Monitoring Satellites (NASA Langley Research Center), Cost–Benefit Analysis of Integrated Energy Facilities (Environmental Protection Agency), Assessment of Hybrid Energy Facilities (National Science Foundation), A Reassessment of the Cross-Florida Barge Canal (Environmental Protection Agency), and Cost–Benefit Analysis of Provincial Investment (Nova Scotia Department of Development). It would be impossible to list everyone whose comments and suggestions improved our work on these projects. However, we feel particularly indebted to Larry Holland, Robert Mason, Terry Ferrar, Ralph D'Arge, George Lawrence, Jim Raper, and T. Truxtun Moebs.

Earlier drafts of this manuscript have been used in our masters-level course in cost–benefit analysis. The comments of our students have measurably improved our exposition.

We owe special gratitude to Ferdinand K. Levy who was Dean of the College of Industrial Management at Georgia Tech during the development of this work. He graciously allowed us time to participate in cost–benefit studies and to allow us to complete our manuscript. He also arranged for the availability of secretarial help and maintained a stimulating academic environment that encouraged and facilitated faculty scholarship. We appreciate the efforts of Sarah Born who was primarily responsible for turning our numerous fragments and revisions into a coherent manuscript. Karen Minnis provided substantial typing as well as proofreading assistance. In addition, Ken Hamilton and Mark Reisenfeld both contributed to the proofreading efforts. Special thanks are due to Marty Arnold for proofreading, for managing the manuscript through the constant flow of corrections and revisions, and for compiling the index. Finally the authors gratefully acknowledge *The Engineering Economist* for permission to use substantial portions of Sassone's Spring 1977 article as the basis for Chapter 4.

COST–BENEFIT ANALYSIS

A Handbook

The legitimate object of government is to do for a community of people whatever they need to have done, but cannot do at all, or cannot do so well themselves, in their separate and individual capacities. In all that the people can individually do as well for themselves, government ought not to interfere.

Abraham Lincoln

1
INTRODUCTION

It is, no doubt, an immense advantage to have done nothing, but one should not abuse it.

Rivarol, Petit Almanach de nos Grands Hommes: Preface

1.1 PURPOSE AND ORGANIZATION

Extensive government expenditures characterize today's economies, both advanced and less advanced. The governments of advanced economies make expenditures on national defense and such diverse social projects as water resource development, transportation networks, manpower training, and technology assessment and transfer. The members of these economies, enjoying a relatively high consumption of goods provided by private enterprise (food, shelter, clothing, etc.), have turned largely to the public sector for further satisfaction of their wants. The governments of the less developed nations, which do not have high standards of living, have determined that one way to achieve prosperity quickly is to develop their "social infrastructures" (communication and transportation systems, pools of skilled labor, education and cultural facilities, etc.). As a result, they take the lead in sponsoring projects to meet these ends. Thus, for varying reasons, public spending is becoming increasingly important around the world. Furthermore, as resource scarcity becomes more severe every year, all governments are compelled to make intelligent choices in the projects they wish to undertake, and of a large number of competing projects, only a few can be chosen for implementation. As public projects are commonly large scale in nature and frequently have irreversible consequences, the need for careful analysis is apparent.

The process of identifying acceptable public projects has become identified with the term *cost–benefit analysis* (CBA).[1] Our purpose in this book is to lay out the fundamentals of CBA in terms useful both to the administrators who request and evaluate project appraisals and to the analysts who perform them. In Chapters 2–9 we deal, respectively, with various decision criteria used in CBA, means of identifying the costs and benefits related to public projects, valuation of costs and benefits, shadow pricing, discount rates, the place of social impact and environmental impact analysis in cost–benefit studies, sensitivity analysis as applied to CBA, and suggestions for organizing and performing a cost–benefit analysis. The remainder of this chapter is devoted to defining cost–benefit analysis and establishing its economic basis.

1.2 DEFINITION

Among noneconomists, "cost–benefit analysis" and "cost-effectiveness analysis" are often erroneously considered to be "techniques" for appraising public projects. If CBA is to be considered "a technique," it is at best a loosely defined one. A "cost–effectiveness analysis" is considered to be a special form or subset of CBA distinguished by the difficulty with which project benefits can be identified in terms of dollars.

---

[1] The term *cost–benefit analysis* (CBA) is used rather than *benefit–cost analysis* to avoid implying that a benefit–cost ratio is either necessary or desirable.

We define a cost-benefit analysis as *an estimation and evaluation of net benefits associated with alternatives for achieving defined public goals*. The meaning or implications of the words in this definition will unfold throughout the reading of this book.

Cost-benefit analysis is a generic term embracing a wide range of evaluative procedures which lead to a statement assessing costs and benefits relevant to project alternatives. The variety of problems addressed and the ingenuity which must be exercised in estimating costs and benefits make it particularly difficult, if not impossible, to design an all-purpose CBA procedure. Several general principles may be stated and a number of guidelines have been established over the years, but public projects differ so much in character that an all-encompassing procedure cannot be defined.

1.3 A BRIEF HISTORY

Although evaluations of public projects have doubtless occurred throughout history, the modern literature on CBA normally dates from 1844 with the publication of an essay, "On the Measurement of the Utility of Public Works," by Jules Dupuit. A French engineer, Dupuit opened his discussion as follows:

> Legislators have prescribed the formalities necessary for certain works to be declared of public utility; political economy has not yet defined in any precise manner the conditions which these works must fulfill in order to be really useful; at least, the ideas which have been put about on this subject appear to us to be vague, incomplete, and often inaccurate. (Dupuit, 1952, p. 83)

When confronted with the task of actually producing a cost-benefit analysis, analysts today feel that they face, at least initially, the same vagueness, incompleteness, and inaccuracies that Dupuit experienced.

Dupuit's most important contribution to economic literature was the idea of *consumer's surplus*,[2] which he presented along with a graphical interpretation. He pointed out that the output of a project multiplied by its price is equal to the minimum social benefit of the project; some consumers might be willing to pay more than the market price and so would enjoy excess utility, or consumer's surplus. This idea led directly to the concept of net social benefit which is now basic to CBA.

While Dupuit's work was the beginning of a stream of thought, we normally consider the application of CBA to have started much later, with the United States Flood Control Act of 1936. By this act, the Congress declared that benefits "to whomsoever they may accrue" of federal projects should exceed costs. But, as observed by Dupuit much before the fact, no consistent methods were developed by which to examine these benefits and costs. The Corps of Engineers, the Soil Conservation Service, the Bureau of Reclamation, and other agencies all used different approaches. With such an accumulation of analytic experience, the Federal Government has attempted to standardize its project-appraisal procedures.

In 1950, the Subcommittee on Benefits and Costs of the Federal InterAgency River Basin Committee issued *Proposed Practices for Economic Analysis of River Basin Projects*. The writers of this document, which is known as the "Green Book," attempted to merge the language of project appraisal and welfare economics. Although the document never achieved official standing, it formed a base for further work and was revised in 1958.

In 1952, the Bureau of the Budget issued its Budget Circular A-47, formally setting forth considerations which would guide the bureau in evaluating proposed projects. Although criticized along with the Green Book for its emphasis on gains as measured by changes in gross national product (GNP) and for ignoring income-distribution issues and gains and losses not measured in

---

[2] Alfred Marshall later gave this name to Dupuit's concept. For a discussion of earlier treatment, see Joseph A. Schumpeter (1954, p. 1061 n).

terms of national income, this circular remained the official guide for project evaluation into the 1960s.

In 1962, Budget Circular A-47 was replaced by Senate Document 97, "Policies, Standards, and Procedures in the Formulation, Evaluation, and Review of Plans for Use and Development of Water and Related Land Resources." After an extended review, this document was replaced in 1973 by "Principles and Standards for Planning Water and Related Land Resources." The latter document represents a substantial revision by the Water Resources Council of Federal practices as established in the 1950s. For example, much more than gains and losses in GNP are now considered. Four accounts are used to display beneficial and adverse effects and to analyze trade-offs among plans: national economic development, environmental quality, regional development, and social well-being. While "plans . . . will be directed to improvement in the quality of life through contributions to the objectives of national economic development and environmental quality" (Water Resources Council, 1973, p. 5), separate accounts are also prepared on regional development and social well-being.

While Federal efforts were directed toward these revisions in practice, a firm theoretical base was being constructed in scholarly circles. Otto Eckstein's (1958) *Water Resources Development* came out of the Harvard University Water Program in 1958, followed by a book of case studies edited by John Krutilla and Eckstein (1958). At the same time Roland N. McKean's (1958) *Efficiency in Government through Systems Analysis* appeared from RAND. These books were quickly followed by others in public expenditure analysis by such scholars as Jack Hirshleifer, J. C. DeHaven, and Jerome W. Milliman (1960), Charles J. Hitch and McKean (1960), Arthur Maass *et al.* (1962), and Robert Dorfman (1965).

In addition to these major critical works, numerous other studies have appeared in almost every field of public expenditure. Several excellent texts are now available on cost–benefit analysis, including those by E. J. Mishan (1976), Ajit K. Dasgupta and D. W. Pearce (1972), and Leonard Merewitz and Stephen H. Sosnick (1971).

1.4   THE ECONOMIC BASIS OF COST–BENEFIT ANALYSIS

Economics is a *social* science dealing with human behavior. Consequently, economics as a science is far less precise than the physical sciences, but perhaps slightly more precise than the other social sciences. In his popular principles of economics text, Paul Samuelson (1973) defined economics as

> the study of how men and society end up choosing, with or without the use of money, to employ scarce productive resources that could have alternative uses, to produce various commodities and distribute them for consumption, now or in the future, among various people and groups in society. It analyzes the *costs and benefits* of improving patterns of resource allocation" (p. 3, italics ours).

The field of economics may be partitioned into *positive* and *normative* areas. Positive economics describes, explains, and predicts actual economic phenomena and is devoid of value judgment. It says nothing about whether given economic states of affairs are good or bad. Normative economics, on the other hand, explicitly introduces value judgments or norms. Its purpose is to assess the relative desirability of different economic states or conditions. Abstractly at least, the method follows a well-accepted two-step paradigm: first, the stipulation of one or several criteria by which to judge states and, second, analyses of the states according to the criteria. Since the decision to implement a public project leads to a change from one economic state to another, and since our desire is certainly to determine which state is "better" (a value judgment), CBA falls directly into the province of normative economics.

The term "normative" is not in common use among economists. Rather, its synonym, "welfare," is the usual term. The reader doubtless has run across allusions to "welfare economics." As happens all too often, the same word has achieved a connotation in the vernacular different from its meaning in economics.

The common *misunderstanding* is to equate welfare economics with so-called government welfare programs, such as the school lunch program or food stamps. Welfare programs are programs which, in some manner, transfer real income from the well-to-do to the less-well-to-do members of society. The welfare-economics approach can be, and is, used to analyze such programs, but welfare economics does *not* espouse such programs. Welfare economics is politically neutral; it is not an apology for political liberalism, and in itself espouses nothing. As a method of analysis (the two-step paradigm mentioned above), it is merely a tool in the hands of the practitioner. The reader who feels that CBA, being related to welfare economics, is somehow politically biased to the left, should note that one of the most common criticisms of CBA is that it ignores income redistribution. That is, the "whomsoever" receiving the benefits of a public project often turns out to be the well-to-do, while the costs often accrue to the less well-to-do. A good CBA will circumvent this pitfall, but if there is any bias at all, it is probably counter to the espousal of welfare programs. In brief, welfare economics, a neutral analytic method, provides the theoretical basis for CBA. Thus, it is sometimes said that CBA is simply applied welfare economics.

If making value judgments about the desirability of economic states is the thrust of welfare economics, its cutting edge is the decision criterion adopted. A welfare economic analysis has merit only insofar as the criterion formulated meets general acceptance. For example, the authors of this manual might suggest the following criterion: Economic State 1 is better for society than Economic State 2 if the authors get more income in State 1 than in State 2. An economic analysis of alternative states based on this criterion is likely to achieve little general acceptance for the simple reason that the preferences of the other members of society are ignored in this criterion. A guiding rule in formulating criteria, at least in Western society, is that each individual's preferences must (somehow) count in the evaluation of alternative economic states. This rule has given rise to four popular criteria: (1) unanimity, (2) Pareto superiority, (3) majority rule, and (4) potential Pareto superiority.

UNANIMITY

Economic state one is to be judged *socially* superior to economic state two if each member of society[3] individually judges one superior to two.

This criterion provokes virtually no dissent. Who can argue that it is not ethical or moral or just? Unfortunately, the criterion is, for all practical purposes, useless. In real life, one will never find a substantive policy issue—a policy which moves the economy from one state to another—on which unanimous agreement can be elicited. In the absence of unanimous agreement, this criterion gives no guidance as to which state is socially better. Thus, it has no value as a guide to policy making.

PARETO SUPERIORITY

Economic State 1 is to be judged *socially* superior to Economic State 2 if at least one person individually judges 1 superior to 2, and no one judges 2 superior to 1. (An Italian engineer-turned-social-scientist, Vilfredo Pareto wrote extensively in economics around the beginning of this century. This criterion is based on his work.)[4]

This criterion amounts to a slight weakening of the previous one—it allows indifference by some individuals when choosing between two states not to affect what is otherwise unanimity. In other words, state 1 is socially superior to state 2 if one or more persons prefer 1 to 2 and everyone else is indifferent. If *only one* person prefers 2 to 1, the criterion breaks down. Nothing then is

---

[3] In practice, the definition of society used in a cost–benefit analysis depends on the particular alternative projects under analysis and may be considered on a local level (for example, a firm or town) or on a macroscopic level, which is the level used in these discussions.

[4] This criterion may be contrasted with the classical welfare criterion which it supplanted. The classical scheme expressed gains and losses in terms of marginal utilities. It required measurement of utility and interpersonal utility comparison, rendering the criterion nonoperational. Pareto's response required neither measurement nor comparison of individual utilities.

said about which state is socially preferable. While economists have long favored this criterion in theoretical discussions, it should be obvious to the reader that such a criterion is a useless policy guide since it will never be applicable. In a real policy choice between two states, preferences on both sides of the issue are bound to exist.

MAJORITY RULE

Economic State 1 is to be judged *socially* superior to Economic State 2 if the majority of the members of society prefer 1 over 2.

The democratic flavor of this criterion suggests that it might be widely acceptable. In fact, of course, it is not employed. Although we may vote for our representatives in government, we do not usually vote directly on policy issues (local referenda would be the exception). Our representatives (those elected or those responsible to elected officials) generally make the policy decisions. Why is this the case? On one level, the answer is simply that this is what government constitutions provide for. On another level, a better answer would be that one could not expect voters to be completely knowledgeable about the hundreds of issues which arise every year. Thus, a policy decision based directly on voting may not be a well-informed decision.

POTENTIAL PARETO SUPERIORITY

Economic State 1 is to be judged *socially* superior to Economic State 2 if those who gain by the choice of 1 over 2 could compensate those who lose so that, if compensation were paid, the final result would be that no one would be worse off than he would be in State 2.[5]

[5] This criterion evolved from Pareto's more limited formulation and a version is sometimes referred to as the Kaldor–Hicks criterion (see Kaldor, 1939, and Hicks, 1939). The Kaldor criterion requires gainers to be able to compensate losers and still be better off; the Hicks criterion requires that loser not be able to profitably bribe gainers not to change. The double criterion was suggested by Scitovsky (1941).

This criterion is more complicated than the previous ones.
An example will serve to clarify it. Suppose only two persons, *A*
and *B*, are affected one way or the other by the movement of the
economy from the status quo to either State 1 or 2. If the change
is to State 1, *A* gains $20 and *B* loses $10. If the change is to State
2, *B* gains $5 and *A* loses nothing. These effects are summarized
in Table 1.1.

According to the criterion, State 1 is socially superior to State
2 because *A* can give *B* an amount of money between $15 and
$20, say $16, so that both end up better off than they would in
State 2. In this case, *A* would end up with $4 (after giving *B* $16
of the $20 gotten in State 1) and *B* ends up with a net gain of $1
(after subtracting *B*'s $15 loss in choosing State 1 over State 2
from *B*'s $16 transfer from *A*). This net potential result is shown
in the last column of Table 1.1. Since no one is worse off than he
would be in State 2, State 1 is socially superior to State 2 by the
Potential Pareto Criterion. Note that if the movement were from
the status quo to State 2, there is no compensation which *B* could
pay *A* to make them both no worse off than they were in State 1.
Thus, the criterion would say, as we would hope, that State 2 is
not socially superior to State 1.

The great advantage that this criterion has over the first two
criteria is that it is always applicable. It is always the case that
the Potential Pareto Criterion, in comparing any two states, will
find one superior to the other, or will find them equal (equality
would have occurred in the example if *B*'s gain from State 2 were
+10 instead of +5, making the aftercompensation result of
choosing either state identical to the other state). In the case of

TABLE 1.1
Illustration of Potential Pareto Superiority

| Person | Gain over status quo | | | Choice of State 1 over State 2 yields: | |
	State 1	State 2	Gross gain	Potential compensation	Net potential gain
A	+20	0	+20	0	+4
B	−10	+5	−15	16	+1

the first two criteria, they simply were not applicable in realistic situations.

A disadvantage of this criterion is that it does not command the universal acceptance that the first two criteria are accorded because the superiority of one state over another is based on a potential, rather than actual, compensation of the losers by the gainers. The criterion does not demand that the compensation actually be paid, only that it is possible that suitable compensation exists to leave no one worse off. There are two defenses to this argument; neither one is completely convincing. First, the progressive tax structure tends to force compensation from gainers to losers. This defense assumes, however, that high earnings are due to public projects financed at the expense of the lower income classes. Second, when a large number of policy decisions are made, losers from one policy will be gainers from another; that is, differences tend to wash out. Empirical evidence in support of these contentions has never been presented, and probably never will be.

The Potential Pareto Criterion forms the basis for the quantitative part of CBA. As is discussed at length later, the qualitative aspects of CBA are attempts to circumvent the lack of universal acceptance to which the criterion is subject.

Looking back at Table 1.1, the reader will appreciate how the Potential Pareto Criterion translates directly into CBA. Cost-benefit analysis is an attempt to ascertain the net benefit (total benefit less total cost) of a policy or project. The net additional benefit of State 1 is +10, while the net additional benefit of State 2 is +5 (20 less 10, and 5 less 0, respectively). A little reflection on the analysis accompanying the example will lead to the appreciation that the difference of $5 in net benefits of State 1 over State 2 was the critical factor in the Potential Pareto Criterion's choice of State 1 over State 2.

In review, cost-benefit analysis is applied welfare economics. The resulting value judgments are frequently based on the Potential Pareto Criterion. In effect, this criterion amounts to choosing the state with the greatest net benefits. Since the Potential Pareto Criterion is not universally accepted as the one and only welfare norm, the quantitative aspects of CBA must be supplemented by qualitative analysis designed to ferret out any socially unacceptable implications that the application of the criterion might entail in any specific circumstance.

1.5 SUMMARY

A cost-benefit analysis identifies and evaluates net benefits associated with alternatives for achieving defined public goals. The techniques used in identifying and comparing cost and benefits are almost as numerous as existing analyses. Nevertheless, some principles and guidelines can be stated.

Cost-benefit analysis is based on Dupuit's concept of consumer's surplus. The art has been developed extensively in planning water-related projects, especially those under Congressional mandate since 1936, and in planning defense systems. A well-established literature on these applications now exists.

As applied welfare economics, cost-benefit analysis uses a decision criterion identified as the Potential Pareto Superiority criterion which labels a project as superior if those who gain from the project could compensate those who lose so that none would be worse off with the project. This criterion identifies net benefits to whomsoever they might accrue and forms the basis for a more detailed review of decision criteria, which is examined in Chapter 2.

2
THE STRUCTURE
OF DECISION PROBLEMS
AND THE CHOICE
OF CRITERIA

We have left undone those things which we ought to have done; and we have done those things which we ought not to have done.

Book of Common Prayer: General Confession

2.1 INTRODUCTION

A sound public decision based on a cost–benefit analysis requires that the analysis be formulated with the appropriate decision criterion in mind. In this chapter we survey the criteria that might be used in making decisions and review the structuring of decision problems.

2.2   A SURVEY OF DECISION CRITERIA

Many criteria have been suggested as appropriate for evaluating alternative investment projects. Some, such as benefit–cost ratios, have a long history of use in cost–benefit analysis and some, such as cutoff and pay-back periods, have been employed only occasionally in public expenditure evaluations. One, however, is considered superior to all the others: net present value. We now present a brief critical review of these criteria, beginning with the one we recommend for most applications.

2.2.1   Net Present Value

The *net present value* (NPV) method reduces a stream of costs and benefits to a single number in which costs or benefits which are projected to occur in the future are "discounted." For example, if a project is expected to yield a benefit worth $100 next year, we might value that $100 next year, as $95 today. There are several reasons for discounting as well as a number of competing arguments as to how the discount *rate* ought to be determined; these are discussed later in Chapter 6. The formula[1] is

$$\text{NPV} = \frac{B_0 - C_0}{(1 + d)^0} + \frac{B_1 - C_1}{(1 + d)} + \cdots + \frac{B_t - C_t}{(1 + d)^t} + \frac{B_n - C_n}{(1 + d)^n},$$

where

C_t is the dollar value of costs incurred at time t,
B_t the dollar value of benefits incurred at time t,
d the discount rate, and
n the life of the project, in years.

The principal problem associated with using the NPV method is

---

[1] The NPV formula is occasionally written with the first term on the right-hand side set at $-C_0$. This reflects a condition where no benefits accrue in the capital-construction period. Obviously no discounting occurs before Year 1.

the determination of the appropriate discount rate. However, as we shall see, this is not a fault of the method itself, and consideration of a *range* of reasonable values is often sufficient in a CBA. Of course, the higher its NPV, the better is a project.

2.2.2 Cutoff Period

Here, a specific time in the future is chosen. A project is acceptable only if it will cover all its costs by that time. Clearly, this method discriminates against projects with benefits that occur some time after the date of inception, even if these benefits are quite substantial. While this method might have its place in a *firm's* profit calculus, especially in risky ventures, it appears to be completely unsuitable for the evaluation of public projects. Society is not faced with a need to earn its investment back quickly; further, we have no good basis for choosing a time period.

2.2.3 Pay-Back Period

According to this criterion, that project which recovers its cost in the shortest period of time is considered best. Its myopia is easily demonstrated. Consider the following comparison of Projects A and B:

Project	C_0	$B_1 - C_1$	$B_2 - C_2$
A	100	110	1
B	100	0	1000

Both A and B involve an initial outlay of 100 and both last two years. Since A returns 110 while B returns nothing after one year, A is judged superior to B. However, considering the second year payoffs, the "pay-back period" judgment certainly appears faulty.[2]

---

[2] The pay-back, or payoff, period, has been used as a decision criterion when use of a discount or interest rate seemed inappropriate. This was the case for

2.2.4 Net Average Rate of Return

The *net average rate* of return (NARR) is defined as the sum of the net benefits over the life of the project divided by the number of years over which such benefits are incured. While overtly reasonable, it has its shortcomings. They are illustrated below:

Project	C_0	$B_1 - C_1$	$B_2 - C_2$	NARR
A	100	115	—	115
B	100	114	114	114

Project *A* lasts one year; Project *B* lasts two years. Using the definition given above, the net average rate of return for each project is easily computed. These are presented in the last column of the table. Note that, although the criterion chooses Project *A* over Project *B*, Project *B* is undisputably superior. The problem, of course, is that with NARR one does not adequately consider the length of the life of a project. Put in another way, with NARR it is implicitly assumed that any project can be done *n* times and will result in an *n*-fold increase in the original net benefits. This assumption is clearly unwarranted in the public sector.

2.2.5 Internal Rate of Return

The *internal rate of return* (IRR) is a measure popularized by John Maynard Keynes and has received a good deal of attention. Until recently, this criterion was considered by many to be as

---

many years in the Soviet Union. Under Marxist doctrine, all value is created by labor and it would be improper to pay a return to capital. With a zero interest rate large-scale capital installations with long-delayed benefits had attractive net present values and were often undertaken despite a serious shortage of capital. When the problems associated with this "gigantomania" were recognized, planners required that a project pay back its initial cost within a specified period of time.

good as the NPV criterion; however, it is now generally regarded as inferior. The IRR of a project is defined as that rate of discounting the future that equates the initial cost and the sum of the future discounted net benefits. That is, the IRR is some r such that

$$C_0 = \frac{B_1 - C_1}{(1 + r)^1} + \cdots + \frac{B_t - C_t}{(1 + r)^t} + \cdots + \frac{B_n - C_n}{(1 + r)^n}.$$

Alternatively, it is the rate r which would make the NPV of the project equal to zero. A project with an IRR exceeding some predetermined level (the social discount rate) is deemed acceptable. Two problems are encountered with this criterion:

(a)   The r that solves the above equation is not necessarily unique. Since the equation is of degree n, it has n roots. Thus, if the social discount rate is 5%, and roots of 3 and 7% are derived as values of r, the interpretation of the IRR is not at all clear.

(b)   The criterion implicitly assumes a single discount rate over the life of the project. Suppose the cost–benefit analyst deems it appropriate to set the social discount rate at 3% for the first x years of the project, and 7% for the remaining $n - x$ years. Again suppose IRR is calculated to be 5%. There is no apparent method for drawing a conclusion about the advisability of the project in such a case.

The internal rate of return and net present value criteria can lead to different conclusions regarding the relative desirability of two projects. This situation is illustrated in Figure 2.1. For two projects, A and B, NPV is plotted as function of the discount rate. The higher the discount rate for either project, the lower the NPV. Let d be the appropriate discount rate for the NPV calculation. Then, according to the figure, A is superior to B by the NPV criterion.

Now, the IRR for each project can be found in the figure by noting where each line crosses the horizontal axis. This is the

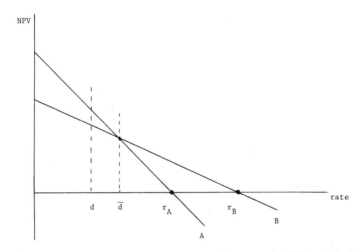

Figure 2.1   Illustration of a possible conflict between the IRR and the NPV rankings of two projects.

discount rate which would make NPV = 0 for that project. The IRRs for the projects are r_A and r_B. Note that r_B is greater than r_A indicating that the IRR criterion suggests project B is superior to project A—the ordering opposite from the NPV criterion.

This situation arises when there exists a rate greater than d which equates the NPVs of A and B at a positive level, that is, when lines A and B cross to the right of d and above the horizontal axis.

What is the implication of this anomaly for project selection? It suggests that the NPV criterion can be made to give conflicting answers at different discount rates. In the figure, for example, $NPV_A > NPV_B$ at d, but $NPV_B > NPV_A$ at r_A. Thus, the differing conclusion of the IRR can be produced by the NPV as well.

Once again, we counsel using the NPV criterion, at the appropriate rate,[3] to resolve any ambiguities between NPV and IRR. For to adopt the conflicting IRR conclusion is tantamount to adopting a different discount rate for NPV.

---

[3] Chapter 6 deals at length with the problems of choosing an appropriate discount rate.

2.2.6   Annual Value

This criterion is formally equivalent to the NPV method. Essentially, it transforms a generally fluctuating *actual* time stream of net benefits (NB) into an NPV-equivalent constant stream. That is, let the actual time stream of net benefits (NB$_i$ = B$_i$ − C$_i$) be

$$NB_0, \quad NB_1, \ldots, NB_t, \ldots, NB_n.$$

The corresponding NPV is

$$NPV = \sum_{t=0}^{n} \frac{NB_t}{(1+d)^t}.$$

Then the *annual value* A is such that

$$\sum_{t=0}^{n} \frac{A}{(1+d)^t} = \sum_{t=0}^{n} \frac{NB_t}{(1+d)^t}.$$

In other words, if A were received every year for n years, the NPV would be the same as when NB$_t$ is received in each of the n years.

2.2.7   Benefit–Cost Ratio

The benefit–cost ratio (B/C) is normally defined in terms of discounted values. The formula for computing the B/C ratio is

$$\frac{B}{C} = \sum_{t=0}^{n} \frac{B_t}{(1+d)^t} \Big/ \sum_{t=0}^{n} \frac{C_t}{(1+d)^t}.$$

While this has been a traditionally popular criterion, it has a fatal flaw when being used to compare two or more projects. Specifically, the benefit–cost ratio gives the (discounted) benefits *per dollar* of (discounted) cost. Thus, the smaller of two projects may have a higher B/C, yet yield a smaller *total* net benefit. An example will clarify this. Two projects, x and y, are being considered for adoption, but only one can be chosen. Each has a life span of one year. Let the discount rate d be 5%. The values required for comparing these two projects are:

Project	B_0	C_0	B_1	C_1	B/C	NPV
x	0	1	2	0	1.9	0.9
y	0	5	8	0	1.5	2.6

As can be seen, x is judged to be superior to y on the B/C criterion, whereas the situation is reversed by NPV. Since y *does* yield a greater increase in society's total net benefits (which is clearly what ought to be maximized), the benefit–cost ratio provides a faulty comparison of projects.

Yet another difficulty in using B/C is its sensitivity to the definition of benefits and the definition of costs. While it would seem that a positive benefit should be identical to a negative cost (of the same magnitude), it clearly makes a difference in the calculation of a ratio whether a sum is added to the numerator or subtracted from the denominator. An application in which this difficulty is likely to surface is in the assessment of external effects, for example, pollution. Is a reduction of pollution a positive benefit to society or a reduction in cost? It is clear from its definition that the NPV criterion suffers from no such ambiguity.

It must be noted, however, that B/C does have a place under certain conditions. This is when several independent projects are to be chosen, given some capital constraint. Then it is appropriate to rank the projects by their respective benefit–cost ratios, implementing successively lower projects until the capital budget is exhausted or until the B/C of the marginal project reaches unity. To see the logic of this approach, consider the following example. There are seven possible projects, A through G. Each has a lifespan of one year, and each incurs only initial costs (that is, no operating costs). Assume a discount rate of 5%, and a capital budget of 5. The relevant information is summarized in Table 2.1.

The NPV and B/C are calculated for each project using their respective formulae presented above. Based on this information,

TABLE 2.1
Hypothetical Example Illustrating the Usefulness of
Benefit–Cost Ratios in Capital-Constrained Choices

Project	Initial cost	Benefits	Net present value	Benefit–cost ratio
A	5	10.50	5.0	2.0
B	1	3.15	2.0	3.0
C	1	4.20	3.0	4.0
D	1	2.63	1.5	2.5
E	1	3.15	2.0	3.0
F	1	2.63	1.5	2.5
G	1	3.15	2.0	3.0

the projects may be ranked by the alternative criteria, NPV and
B/C, as follows:

Project ranking by NPV	Project ranking by B/C
A	C
C	B, E. G
B, E, G	D, F
D, F	A

Under each criterion, the projects are ranked top to bottom, and
those on the same level are equal according to the criterion.
Looking first at the NPV ranking, the budget of 5 dictates that
only the top-ranked project, A, could be implemented since A
exhausts the capital budget. The net benefits accruing to society
from A are given by A's NPV, which is 5. Turning to the B/C
ranking, Project C, Projects B, E, or G, and Projects D or F, all of
which are smaller, would be implemented. These exhaust the
capital budget, and the sum of their NPVs is 10.5. Thus, we see
that in order to maximize the total (or sum of) NPV over several
independent projects, subject to a capital constraint, the rule is to
adopt projects based on the B/C ranking.

2.2.8   Minimum Average Cost

This criterion addresses the scale question. It is based on the assumption that the optimum scale of a project is that scale which minimizes average cost. The criterion is unequivocally *incorrect* for the simple reason that, by focusing exclusively on costs, it takes no account of benefits. In fact, the proper scale criterion is to set the scale so that marginal cost equals marginal benefit. This correct criterion, and its relation to the minimum average cost criterion, is readily illustrated with graphs common to microeconomics, as shown in Figure 2.2. We assume, for

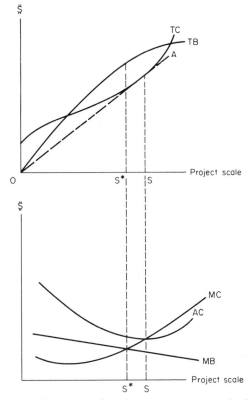

Figure 2.2   Illustration of minimum-average-cost criterion.

expositional purposes, that scale is a continuous variable. The upper graph depicts total cost (TC) and total benefit (TB) as functions of scale, the lower graph presents marginal cost (MC), marginal benefit (MB), and average cost (AC).

Looking first at the "total" graph, we see that minimum average cost occurs at scale S. (Graphically, the average value at any point on a curve is the slope of the ray from the origin to that point. Here the ray OA is clearly the least steep such ray; hence, S is minimum-average-cost scale.) However, note that net benefits (TB $-$ TC) are maximized, not at S, but at S^*, the scale at which MB and MC intersect. This is a graphic statement of the following condition from the calculus: to maximize net benefits (a function of scale), the first derivative of net benefits must be equated to zero.

2.2.9 Equity

This criterion addresses the impact of the benefits and costs of a project on the individual members (or groups or classes) of society. On the most abstract level, the equity issue can never be adequately resolved by economic reasoning because at its heart is the moral or ethical issue of how to compare the relative importance (or value) of different persons. Is "social welfare" unchanged if we take $100 from one person and give it to another? The answer might be that it depends on the individuals—their incomes, their wealth, their expenses, etc. No rule can be developed that adequately covers every circumstance. However, virtually all economists agree that a project which *benefits only* the rich and *costs only* the poor should be judged inferior, *ceteris paribus*, to the converse situation. Of course, almost any project will benefit some rich and poor alike and cost some rich and poor alike. Thus, the above criterion hardly provides a complete equity-decision criterion.

With regard to the equity issue, then, the way to proceed is *not* to incorporate a formal "equity function" into the NPV maximand (since any such function is highly arbitrary). Rather, any cost–benefit analysis should include a separate, detailed statement as to how the costs and benefits of the project will be distributed among the members of society. In the final analysis, the decision maker must subjectively weigh the NPV of a project against any adverse equity consequences. Such a subjective weighing will necessarily reflect the decision maker's own ethical standards, and possibly political realities as well.

The argument is made by many economists that mildly adverse equity consequences ought not *necessarily* preclude the acceptance of a project since, at any time, a number of diverse projects are likely being undertaken by a variety of government agencies. Furthermore, so the argument goes, distributional (equity) consequences are likely to be self-canceling. It should be noted, however, that there is no empirical substantiation for this assumption.

Another argument in support of the contention that mildly adverse equity consequences not preclude a project is that there are far better means of achieving a given distribution of benefits and costs among society than by choosing public projects to that end. Adjustment of income tax rates, for example, is a far more flexible and accurate tool. Thus, in principle, an identifiable group of individuals who are repeatedly hurt by public projects could be compensated by more favorable tax treatment. Once again, however, we can offer no assurance that this does, or would, actually occur.

2.3 THE STRUCTURE OF DECISION PROBLEMS

2.3.1 Alternative Decision Forms

Once a social objective and the alternative means (projects) by which it might be achieved are precisely and explicitly defined (no mean task), it will be found that the structure of the decision problem takes one of three mutually exclusive forms:

(1) One project is to be accepted or rejected.
(2) One of several candidate projects is to be accepted.
(3) Several of many candidate projects are to be accepted.

The first two forms are relatively simple and require little discussion. But the last form, choice of several projects, has some special aspects. In particular, it is important to determine whether the projects are independent or dependent and whether there is an effective capital constraint limiting the sum of initial expenditures on the group of selected projects.

2.3.2 Project Interdependence

The independent–dependent issue demands some clarification. *A project is independent of other projects if the net present value (NPV) of that project is invariant with respect to whether or not any of the other projects are implemented and with respect to the scale of those projects.* Projects are independent of each other as long as the above criterion is satisfied for each project. Implied by this definition is that, for a group of independent projects, the NPV of any one project is unambiguously given by a scalar number (not by conditional relations), and the NPV of any subgroup of projects is simply the sum of the NPV scalars of each of those projects. A project is dependent on other projects if the above italicized criterion is not satisfied.

For example, suppose public beaches are being considered for development along a stretch of coastline. The stretch is 60 miles long, and 6 million persons live along it, evenly distributed along its entire length. There are three possible sites (A, B, C) for the beaches, at the 10-, 30-, and 50-mile points along its expanse, and 0, 1, 2, or 3 sites are to be developed as beaches. The NPV of a beach is $50 to an individual if he does not have to travel to reach it. Traveling reduces its value by $1 per mile. Thus, an

individual values a beach 8 miles away at $42. However, the
same individual values a beach 50 miles away at 0 since he would
never use it. Each site, if developed, will be in every way equal.
The cost of development is $50 million per site. The questions
addressed by the cost–benefit analysis is which site(s) to develop, if any.

Let us now determine the benefits associated with a beach at
Site A. Clearly, all persons west of A will use that beach, and the
sum of net present value for those individuals is $45 million (M)
(average benefit of $45 per person times number of persons). All
persons east of Site A will not necessarily use that facility. If Site
B is developed, only persons west of the 20-mile point will use A,
since B is closer for all others. If C, but not B, in addition to A is
developed, only persons living west of the 30-mile point will use
A. Therefore, the benefits associated with A are *not* invariant
with respect to whether the other projects are implemented. The
calculations for A must be presented in tabular form—benefits
cannot be unambiguously expressed by a single scalar. Such a
table takes the form shown in Table 2.2. All the foregoing should
make quite clear what is meant by independence, or the lack of
it, among projects.

By continuing the example a bit further, another crucial
point can be illustrated. When projects are dependent, the only
proper way to proceed is to form all possible (or economically
feasible, if there is an effective capital constraint) combinations
of projects, and to evaluate the NPV of each such combination.
The combination with the greatest NPV is to be selected for

TABLE 2.2
Benefits Associated with Site A in a Hypothetical
Beach Development

Site(s) developed	Benefits from A
A alone	$170 M
A and B	$90 M
A and C	$125 M
A, B, and C	$90 M

TABLE 2.3
Calculation of Net Benefits Associated with Alternative Project
Combinations in Hypothetical Beach Development

Projects	Present value of benefits	Present value of costs	Net present value
None	$0	$0	$0
A	$170 M	$50 M	$120 M
B	$210 M	$50 M	$160 M
C	$170 M	$50 M	$120 M
A, B	$240 M	$100 M	$140 M
A, C	$250 M	$100 M	$150 M
A, B, C	$270 M	$150 M	$120 M

implementation. For this example, there are seven possible combinations. The relevant decision table is shown in Table 2.3. Site *B*, resulting in the greatest NPV, is the correct choice. Note that the *dependence* of the projects is clearly apparent in the table. The NPV of any combination of projects is not equal to the sum of NPV for the individual projects.

2.3.3 Capital Constraints

One point frequently omitted from superficial discussions of public expenditures is the relative scarcity of funds. This is especially true of situations in which positive decisions are based on a benefit–cost ratio (B/C) greater than one, for example, in many congressional decisions on water resource projects. But, whether implicit or explicit, capital constraints always exist, and this decision criterion is of very limited value.[4]

---

[4] In fact, the usefulness of an acceptance criterion of B/C greater than one is so small that the term (benefit–cost analysis) is not commonly used primarily to avoid the restrictive implications of B/C ratios.

2.3.4   A Formal Decision Tree

We are now prepared to present the formal decision tree matching each problem structure with the appropriate decision criterion. This tree is presented in Figure 2.3.

To illustrate use of the tree, let us look at the foregoing beach development example, which involved the choice of a few (which, for our purposes, simply means that the choice was not restricted to no more than one) projects; they were clearly dependent, and we assumed that there was no capital constraint. Hence, we listed each possible combination, and chose the one with maximum NPV. Had there been a capital constraint of, say, $100 M, our feasible sets would have excluded (*A*, *B*, *C*). In this case, the final choice would not have been altered. It is not difficult, of course, to envision circumstances wherein the imposition of a financial constraint *would* alter the project choice.

The rest of the decision tree is intuitively clear, except

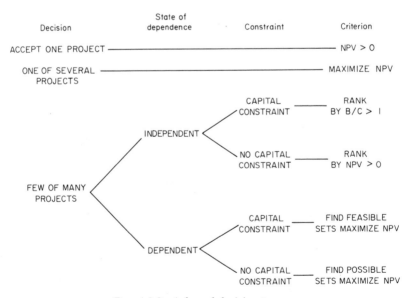

Figure 2.3   A formal decision tree.

perhaps, for the solitary mention of the benefit-cost ratio crite-rion. On the branch for which a few projects are to be selected that are subject to a capital constraint, ranking by B/C (and choosing accordingly!) is equivalent to maximizing the sum of the NPVs over all feasible sets of projects.

2.4 SUMMARY

This section has been devoted to fundamentals. The net present value criterion is generally accepted as the proper deci-sion criterion to be used in cost-benefit analysis. It is preferred in contrast to annual value because of its clarity and to a benefit-cost ratio because of its superiority and general applicability. In this section we also reviewed the several forms of decision problems, identifying the problems associated with project inter-dependence and capital constraints.

3
IDENTIFYING
COSTS AND BENEFITS

> Why does this magnificent applied science which saves work and
> makes life easier bring us so little happiness? The simple answer runs:
> Because we have not yet learned to make sensible use of it.
>
> Albert Einstein, *Address,* California Institute of Technology
> February 1931

3.1 THE IDENTIFICATION PROBLEM

Once the project has been clearly defined, the next major
problem in performing a cost–benefit analysis is to properly
identify costs and benefits. This is true for several reasons. The
choice of a decision criterion is simple since it is normally
dictated by the problem structure. Measurement is merely tedi-
ous when it is possible and, although frustrating, hardly a
problem when it is impossible. Once the researcher has a clear
grasp of the procedures involved, sensitivity analysis becomes
relatively easy. Also, some very difficult philosophical questions,
such as the choice of a proper discount rate, are often resolved by
a political decree. However, defining the analytic task, or objec-

31

tives, and identifying the detailed categories of costs and benefits and the other questions to be resolved in the course of a study are really major tasks that demand clear thought and careful planning.

At the outset it should be pointed out that a major stumbling block in identifying costs and benefits is the double-counting problem. Much of the criticism levied against early CBAs and much of the nontechnical controversy in the literature has concerned the counting of benefits more than once, usually in an attempt to cover all possible objectives for a project.

In assessing the benefits and costs of a project, benefits and costs may be classified in several ways, and classificatory schemes can be both useful and harmful. They are harmful in that various categories overlap with others and may frequently lead to confusion and double counting. On the other hand, they are useful in that classification is an aid to identifying effects, and knowledge of the various classificatory schemes can eliminate such problems as double counting. One obvious example of a classificatory scheme is that of "benefit and costs," which divides the effects of a project into positive effects (benefits) and negative ones (costs). In the remainder of this section we present a discussion of the various classifications of benefits and costs that appear in the literature and conclude with some general remarks on developing a scenario for CBA. Throughout the section it is important to realize that, although it may be desirable to place a benefit in one category or another, the important thing is that benefits (costs) be additions (deletions) to the real product of an economy.

3.2 CLASSIFICATORY SCHEMES

3.2.1 Internal versus External Effects

Internal benefits accrue directly or indirectly to the entity under study. In the simplest case, the benefits returned by a private investment would be the revenues produced. For social investment, internal benefits might properly be construed as those increases in values produced directly by the project itself as well as secondary increases in welfare occurring in other parts of the social entity. The domain of a project is commonly restricted to the project itself, and internal benefits are those "captured" by the project.

External effects are much more complex in definition. External benefits "escape" the project and fall into the hands of others. Although these benefits may be valued, they cannot be priced. The quantity of external effects may vary with the size of the decision unit. For example, a private hydroelectric dam may render flood control benefits to outsiders living downstream; these are external benefits. But a dam constructed by the Corps of Engineers on behalf of the United States may render flood control benefits to citizens of the United States. To avoid undue controversy, externalities should be defined with reference to the project itself, and the proper definitional question should be whether the benefits can be captured, priced, and sold by the project entity.

External benefits thus may be defined as benefits involuntarily received by others for which they pay nothing. External costs are similarly defined as costs imposed on others without compensation. Collectively, these external effects are often called *externalities*. They are neither deliberately produced nor deliberately consumed.

Externalities may be classified as either technological or pecuniary.[1] *Technological externalities* involve changes in *real* consumption or production opportunities for outsiders. Thus, increased recreational opportunities and flood controls associated with a private hydroelectric dam are technological externalities. These externalities represent increased social welfare, cannot easily be priced, and are produced incidental to the purpose of the dam. Most frequently, technological externalities result from joint products.

Pecuniary externalities are associated with the *financial* effects

---

[1] This distinction was made by Tibor Scitovsky (1954).

of the project on others, as felt through price changes for outputs or inputs. Thus, decreases in the price of a product itself, increases in the price of a complement, decreases in the price of a substitute, decreases in the price of a joint product, or increases in the price of a resource used in production are all pecuniary externalities.

Technological externalities clearly should be accounted for in a cost–benefit analysis—they are real and they increase or decrease social welfare. Pecuniary externalities normally should be excluded: they most likely represent redistribution of income, and their inclusion would represent double counting. For example, a rapid-transit station may increase the mobility of a nearby resident, yielding great time savings. The value of such time saving is real and should be counted; the increased value of a resident's house is pecuniary and should not be counted since it is derived from the real time-saving gain.

3.2.2 Incommensurables and Intangibles

Incommensurables are effects which "cannot readily be translated into the common denominator or denominators that are being used" (Hitch and McKean, 1960, p. 182). *Intangibles* are incommensurables that are not measurable in even their own terms.

Use of the term "incommensurable" has been questioned by Dasgupta and Pearce (1972), who point out that "logically, there can be no such thing as an 'incommensurable' good. By definition of the concept of a shadow price . . . , every outcome has a social opportunity cost, and hence a shadow price" (p. 113). These authors prefer the term "intangible" as descriptive of effects ". . . in which there is no market, or in which there is reason to suppose that existing markets do not value an effect completely" (Dasgupta and Pearce, 1972, p. 112).

The distinction between incommensurables and intangibles is important. Although incommensurables might technically not exist, if "cannot *readily* be translated" be emphasized in the definition, then the set of effects to which the shadow pricing question applies has been isolated. The real problem in CBA is in developing adequate measures for this category of effects. The term "intangible" can be reserved for the really unmeasurable effects.

A useful distinction of these "extramarket" effects might be between

> ". . . those of a material or economic nature and those involving values beyond the economic. Thus the provision of recreation facilities is obviously economic in nature in that additional commodities or services are made available to the public; it is . . . [incommensurable] solely because of difficulties of measurement which are not, as a matter of fact, completely intractable. The preservation of human life or of democratic processes, on the other hand, brings, into account values beyond the economic" (Hirshleifer *et al.*, 1960, p. 132).

With these remarks in mind, we prefer to use the term "incommensurable" to refer to all extramarket effects, reserving "intangible" to describe qualitative terms that are noneconomic in nature.

The analyst may be tempted to ignore incommensurables in an effort to compile a single dollar-value number for net benefits or a single benefit–cost ratio. This could very well be a mistake, for the effects of incommensurables could be just as important as others. When decision makers choose between alternatives, they implicitly value the incommensurables; analysts simply face the problem of having no generally accepted procedure for quantitatively integrating these terms into their analyses and of presenting an analysis with marred neatness.

An example might be seen in comparing two projects for orbiting manned spaceships. One is more expensive in dollars but includes multiple backup and recovery systems which minimize possible losses of lives while the other is less expensive in dollars but has a higher probability associated with losses of lives. These alternatives cannot readily be expressed in common terms, yet they both must be considered by the decision maker.

Other examples of incommensurables include human life, air pollution, noise, national defense, scenic or historic sites, public recreation facilities, public transportation benefits, prestige, social institutions, and redistribution of production or consumption (net of efficiency).

Incommensurables can be treated in cost–benefit studies in several ways. Although considered more thoroughly in the discussion of shadow pricing (Chapter 5), several alternatives deserve mention. One approach is simply to ignore the values of incommensurables; but this approach is obviously hazardous, even wrong. The decision maker has a very inadequate notion of alternatives and, in fact, must know the values of effects not counted to know the importance of values included. At the very least, the analyst should list, or possibly describe, all effects which are not quantitatively evaluated in his analysis. Another approach may be to identify effects in terms of physical (or other) units. If the number of measures is small enough, the decision maker may then have adequate information to properly weigh alternatives. This approach may also be sufficient to suggest an alternative valuation scheme to the analyst.

In the case of public goods for which shadow prices cannot be constructed, the cost–benefit analysis may become a cost-effectiveness analysis (CEA), which in essence is a CBA with benefits not defined in the same terms as costs. Thus, the objective may become maximizing physical benefits subject to a cost constraint, or it may become minimizing costs for a given level of physical benefits, or, in the case of an intangible, for a given benefit. For example, consider the provision of equal access to public facilities for all citizens, including the handicapped and aged. "Equality of access" is an intangible benefit that cannot be quantified. The CBA, or CEA, would then compare alternatives for achieving this goal.

The value of an incommensurable may also be estimated in terms of alternatives. For example, suppose that alternative A is associated with considerable incommensurables while B is not. Alternative A might be a domed stadium to house numerous major league activities lending substantial prestige to a city while B might be park and recreation facilities estimated to yield equivalent recreational benefits to city residents. Other things being equal, for the city to prefer the stadium to the parks it must, at a minimum, value the prestige as the difference in the costs of the two projects. By casting a decision to build or not to build a stadium in terms of alternatives, the analyst at least permits the decision maker to see the values that must be placed on incommensurables for a positive decision.

Shadow prices may be assigned in several ways. Values of similar goods in private markets, the results of consumer surveys, prices implicit in historic governmental decisions, and the like may be used as proxies for a market price for incommensurables. These problems are discussed in detail in Chapter 5.

The important point, then, is that incommensurables be displayed and discussed. Even if valued, they might best be considered separately to emphasize their nonmarket nature.

3.2.3 Direct versus Indirect Effects

A direct benefit of a project is simply defined as an increased real value of output associated with the project. The most common direct benefit would be greater physical production: more grain from an irrigation project, more power from a hydroelectric dam, etc. Direct benefits may also arise from changes in quality (for example, development of a higher grade turkey), in temporal value (for example, from storage facilities), in spatial value (for example, from transportation facilities), or in form (for example, from sorting fruit). The important point is that either output increases or the demand curves of consumers increase, leading to an increase in consumer's surplus.

Secondary or indirect benefits "reflect the impact of the project on the rest of the economy" (Eckstein, 1958, p. 202). The term is normally applied to "the increased incomes of various producers . . . that stem from . . . projects" (McKean, 1958, p. 154). Its use has been severely criticized because of the doubtful applicability of the concept.[2]

---

[2] To our knowledge, the best criticisms of the use of secondary benefits are found in Eckstein (1958, pp. 202–214) and McKean (1958, pp. 151–167).

Secondary benefits are a form of external benefits. The term has been used primarily to identify incomes "stemming from" or "induced by" a project. Benefits stemming from a project include the net incomes of processors between the primary product and consumers (for example, the merchants, haulers, millers, and bakers lying between grain producers and consumers). This notion is much akin to the concept of "forward linkages" used in development economics. Benefits induced by a project are related in the same vein to the concept of "backward linkages" and represent a counting of incomes of firms that supply inputs to primary producers. Because of the nature of these trackings, economic multipliers have been used occasionally to estimate secondary benefits.

But the validity of tracking such benefits has been severely questioned and it is important to understand the criticisms levied against users of the category, primarily the Corps of Engineers. In an economic analysis of agricultural projects, J. P. Gittinger (1972) has summarized "... the conditions under which the full multiple-effects ... constitute a real net change in welfare ..." (p. 27). These conditions include:

(1) the public expenditure is not financed out of tax revenues so that the multiplier-creating expenditures are not drawn away from the private sector;

(2) the conditions of supply for all factors stimulated to employment by the investment are perfectly elastic at prevailing prices;

(3) the opportunity costs of those factors in the absence of the investment are zero; and

(4) the outputs which result do not simply substitute for other products in the market place and, thus, do not result in unemployment for other factors of production. (Gittinger, 1972, p. 27)

It is obvious that these conditions could seldom apply, especially in the long time period over which most cost–benefit analyses normally apply.

Eckstein summarizes the arguments from a national viewpoint against considering indirect benefits as follows:

> . . . stemming benefits are very unlikely in depres-
> sion, are a possibility during inflation if the specific
> commodities are in particularly short supply, and can
> only be granted for periods of economic balance in those
> instances where the premise of mobility can be denied
> because of extraordinary circumstances. The routine
> calculation of stemming benefits, therefore, is not war-
> ranted.
> . . . induced benefits, on the other hand, are largely
> confined to the construction of the project. They are
> large in times of depression, nonexistent in times of
> economic balance, and negative during inflation.
> . . . it can . . . only be concluded that the use of
> indirect benefits in benefit-cost analysis must be con-
> fined to cases where it can be shown that there are
> unemployed and immobile resources or that there is
> underutilized capacity in associated economic activities.
> (Eckstein, 1958, pp. 211-212)

Perhaps the most violent attack on the counting of secondary
benefits has come from McKean. In an exhausting presentation,
McKean (1958, Chapter 8), points out the clear arguments against
counting secondary effects in a fully employed economy, as
above, and goes on to question the usefulness of the concept
under conditions of unemployment. Not only must involuntary
unemployment or underemployment exist for secondary employment benefits to be counted, but the condition must have
otherwise existed for the entire project period. The hazards and
uncertainties associated with projecting long-term resource unemployment are such that measurement of secondary benefits in
a national cost-benefit analysis is not warranted.

From a regional point of view, the estimation of secondary
benefits is less risky since the "openness" of a regional economy
lessens the constraints on resource use. But the important question here is not in counting benefits but in defining objectives. If
the objective of the project is regional development, or spatial

redistribution of economic activity, then secondary benefits may be real and important and should at least be identified and listed (although inclusion in a formal summation of benefits is still open to question). Arthur Maass (1966) succinctly summarizes this point as follows:

> . . . it is interesting to examine the arguments over so-called secondary benefits and how they should be included, if at all, in project analyses. There is no such thing as a secondary benefit. A secondary benefit, as the phrase has been used in the benefit-cost literature, is in fact a benefit in support of an objective other than efficiency. The word benefit (and the word cost, too) has no meaning by itself, but only in association with an objective; there are efficiency benefits, income redistribution benefits, and others. Thus, if the objective function for a public program involves more than economic efficiency—and it will in most cases—there is no legitimate reason for holding that the efficiency benefits are primary and should be included in the benefit-cost analysis whereas benefits in support of other objectives are secondary and should be mentioned, if at all, in separate subsidiary paragraphs of the survey report. Using the current language and current standards, most of the benefits to the Indians in the Indian irrigation project are secondary benefits. How silly! (p. 211)

3.3 DEVELOPING A SCENARIO

With some of the problems associated with identifying costs and benefits in mind it is worthwhile to introduce now the concept of a scenario. How does one go about developing a scenario for analysis? This question is briefly commented on here, and is discussed in more detail in Chapter 9.

The first step in developing a scenario is to identify the

objective of a public expenditure. If, for example, a dam is to be built, is the real objective to increase recreation alternatives, control flooding, and produce electric power in a river basin? Or is the objective to build a dam justified by contributions to social welfare through serving several objectives? Can the objective(s) be separated from the means (the dam, itself)? The analyst may work under a restrictive mandate from a public authority and so be limited in the pursuit of alternative means; in this case, alternatives may be investigated by other interest groups. Or the analyst may be charged with examining all possibilities. Therefore, the first question to be settled is: What are the objectives of, and alternatives to, a project?

Once this question is settled, a set of accounts must be devised through which to organize the analysis. This process is based on experience and observation and, to some extent, public law.[3] Federal projects, for example, require both national economic development and environmental accounts, with distributional accounts (such as regional development or income–class) displayed for information. After the summary accounts are established, then the analyst must identify the benefits and costs appearing under each account and carefully check for double-counting problems.

---

[3] The best source of information on setting up accounts is the "Principles, Standards, and Procedures for Water and Related Land Resource Planning" (Water Resources Council, 1973) and the critical literature associated with this document.

4
QUANTIFYING COSTS AND BENEFITS

Eodem animo beneficium debetur, quo datur. . . . Beneficium non in eo quod fit aut datur consistit, sed in ipso dantis aut facientis animo. (A benefit is estimated according to the mind of the doer. . . . It consists not in what is done, but in what is intended.) Seneca, *De Beneficiis, Book:, section 4*

Beneficium invito non datur. (A benefit cannot be bestowed on an unwilling person.)

4.1 INTRODUCTION

It is fair to state that the most important aspect of a cost–benefit analysis is the *identification* of all the relevant costs and benefits. Second only to this in importance is the quantification of such costs and benefits. The *raison d'être* of quantification is to facilitate the analyzing of trade-offs. Any CBA will involve considerations of both losses and gains to society. Obviously, the magnitudes of such losses and gains are crucial to the decision maker.

It is not enough in cost–benefit analysis to describe effects of a project as harsh, or slight, or moderate, or whatever. Rather, as much as possible, it is important to quantify impacts. Only through quantification is the aggregation of effects and the analysis of trade-offs generally possible. This chapter first introduces the two postulates that provide the philosophical basis for valuation in CBA. It shows that market prices, under a wide variety of circumstances, satisfy these postulates as measures of value. In this context, a formal framework for CBA is developed. Finally the concept of "shadow price" is introduced and the relation between market prices and shadow prices is explored as a preliminary to the more detailed presentation in Chapter 5.

4.2   VALUATION PHILOSOPHY

In CBA, the monetary valuation of project effects rests on two fundamental postulates:

POSTULATE I

The social value of a project is the sum of the values of the project to the individual members of society.

POSTULATE II

The value of a project to an individual is equal to his (fully informed[1]) *willingness to pay* for the project.

Postulate I rejects an organic view of the state, in which the society is seen as more than the collection of individuals who comprise it. Thus, a project can never be justified in CBA by appeal to "the good of the state" where that "good" is not identical with the "good" to the individual members of the state.

Postulate II sanctions both consumer sovereignty and the existing distribution of income. Consumer sovereignty implies

---

[1] Willingness to pay can be a useful measure of social value only if the individual's willingness to pay is based on a knowledge of the relevant aspects of the project.

that the individual is the best judge of his own welfare, or state of well-being. Thus, when we speak of the *value* of a project to an individual in a CBA, that value is computed with specific reference to the consumer's own judgments as to the worth of a good. Consumer sovereignty is to be contrasted with a "dictatorial regime" wherein the decision maker is allowed to base his decision on how he feels one should value a good. By way of example, suppose that the market price of a "baked Alaska" is $3 and a project will reduce their production by 100 units. Consumer sovereignty demands that we value that decrease as a cost of $300 to society, however much the decision maker feels that we are all too fat and that fewer baked Alaskas are not a loss at all, or even a gain.

To see that income distribution affects prices, thereby potentially affecting the results of a CBA, consider the following example. A project being evaluated by CBA has a social cost of $5000. Its only benefit will be an increase in the output of walking canes, the kind used exclusively by retired persons (whose average income is notoriously low). The current market price of these canes is $7. The projected increase in output is 600 canes. The market value of the benefits is $4200. The net social benefits are −$800. If retired persons had higher incomes, the market demand curve for canes would lie to the right. Assuming that the long-run supply curve of canes is upward sloping, the result would be a higher market price for canes—say, $9 each. The net social benefits are now +$400. If the decision maker bases a judgment entirely on the CBA, the distribution of income is the critical factor. Paradoxically, higher income qualifies the retired persons to get more benefits. The point here, then, is that for a decision maker to reject the project because it lost $800, he must implicitly sanction the existing income distribution.

4.3   MARKET PRICES AS A MEASURE OF SOCIAL VALUE

Let us now investigate how market prices are, indeed, empirical manifestations of willingness to pay. Consider an

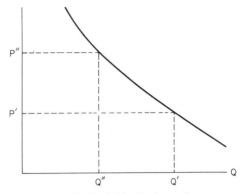

Figure 4.1   An individual's demand curve.

individual's demand curve for some commodity Q, as shown in
Figure 4.1. Quantity (Q) is measured along the horizontal axis
and price (P) along the vertical axis. The demand curve shows the
quantities of the commodity the individual is willing and able to
purchase (per time period) at each price. For example, if the
market price is P'', the individual will purchase Q'', and if the
market price were P', Q' would be purchased. For each unit of Q
purchased, the rational individual must subjectively determine
whether the value of that unit to himself exceeds the cost. Since it
is generally true that successive units of any commodity have less
and less value to an individual,[2] as the individual continues to
consider additional units for purchase, he eventually reaches a
unit for which the value to himself is less than the cost. Clearly,
the rational individual will not purchase a unit of a commodity if
the value of the marginal unit is less than its cost. In general, as
long as the commodity is sufficiently divisible, the rational
individual will purchase a specific number of units such that the
value of the marginal unit is just equal to the cost of the marginal
unit. To buy either more or less than that number is suboptimal,
since a change in the number purchased (toward the number at
which the marginal equality is achieved) increases the well-being
of the individual by increasing the positive difference between

---

[2] In the jargon of economics, this is "diminishing marginal utility."

the total value of goods consumed and the total cost of those goods. Willingness to pay is the objective manifestation of the value an individual ascribes to a commodity.

Now suppose the price of the commodity is P', and the consumer purchases Q' units. What is his willingness to pay for the Qth unit? Surely it cannot be less than P', for if it were, he would not have purchased that unit. Equally, it cannot be much greater than P', for if it were, he would have purchased more than Q' units (until the marginal value equals the marginal cost). It follows that his willingness to pay is just P'. Thus, we have a fundamental conclusion of microeconomics:

> *Faced with any given price for a commodity, the rational individual, in seeking to advance his state of well-being as much as possible, will purchase a number of units of that commodity so that, at the margin, his willingness to pay for that commodity is just equal to its price.*

It follows that if one of the effects of a project were a small increase or decrease in the number of units of a commodity available to an individual for consumption, that increase or decrease has a social value equal to the number of units involved times the market price.

4.4 A FORMAL CBA FRAMEWORK

We are now prepared to introduce the formal framework and some terminology of CBA. A *state* (of the world) S is a specific distribution of utility[3] among the members of society; that is,

$$S = (U^1, U^2, \ldots, U^j, \ldots, U^N)$$

[3] The utility function reflects all of the decision maker's feelings about various events and may well include factors other than monetary factors. For an interesting discussion of the distinction between a government objective function and a social welfare function, see Nash *et al.* (1975).

for a society of N members. A *project* is a well-defined, intentional action or set of actions that will lead society from the *status quo* (current state) S^0 to alternative state S'. The *value of a project* to individual j, V_j, is the maximum amount he would be willing to pay to have the project adopted when he favors the project and is the negative of the minimum amount he would accept as payment in order to remain just as well off in S' as in S^0 when he does not favor the project. When the project does not alter j's utility, $V_j = 0$. (Economists have a special term for V_j: *compensating variation*.) The social value of a project V is

$$\sum_{j=1}^{n} V_j.$$

That is, social value is based on willingness to pay of individuals. This is the basic and straightforward principle of measurement in CBA.

Now, how is V to be inferred? Asking each and every individual for his V_j is clearly a hopeless task for two reasons. First, each person would have to be apprised of every detail of the project and its consequences so that he could come to some conclusion about its value to himself. This alone would appear to be a practical impossibility. Second, there is no reason to suppose that every person would convey his true V_j, particularly if it were negative. The tendency would be to overstate one's distaste for the project in the hope of influencing the final decision.

Thus, the V_j's are best determined without recourse to interviews or questionnaires. As discussed above, and subject to a number of qualifications discussed later, market prices reflect the V_j's.

Suppose that the only effects of a project are an increase in the production of good X by ΔX and a decrease in the production of good Y by ΔY. The prices of the goods P_x and P_y remain unchanged. The value of the project to individual j is

$$V_j = P_x \, \Delta X_j - P_y \, \Delta Y_j,$$

where ΔX_j and ΔY_j are changes in consumption of X and Y by individual j. Clearly,

$$\Delta X = \sum_{j=1}^{n} \Delta X_j$$

$$\Delta Y = \sum_{j=1}^{n} \Delta Y_j.$$

To find the social value of the project directly, by summing the V_j's, is an onerous task. It involves knowing each ΔX_j and each ΔY_j. The job is greatly simplified by noting that

$$V = \sum_{j=1}^{n} V_j$$

$$= \sum_{j=1}^{n} (P_x \, \Delta X_j - P_y \, \Delta Y_j)$$

$$= P_x \sum_{j=1}^{n} \Delta X_j - P_y \sum_{j=1}^{n} \Delta Y_j$$

$$= P_x \, \Delta X - P_y \, \Delta Y.$$

Thus, CBA conclusions can be reached from knowledge of the gross physical effects (ΔX and ΔY) and the corresponding market prices of those goods.

Thus, we have the basis for the meaningful aggregation of project effects across individuals and across different effects. In principle, aggregation is a potentially overwhelming difficulty, for a single metric (or yardstick) must be used against grossly varied circumstances. Fortunately, price is the single thread which draws the many different project effects under the same valuation principle.

The conclusion also produces a tremendous economy in requisite information. Rather than having to elicit valuation information from each affected individual, a task ranging from expensive to astronomical, the analyst finds the necessary information, market prices, at his fingertips. A related corollary is that cost and benefit determinations may be based only on a knowledge of the gross physical effects of a project, independent of a knowledge of the distribution of the effects among the members of society.[4]

4.5   SHADOW PRICES

The term "shadow price" has received a good deal of attention in recent years. Two circumstances account for this. First, the so-called "dual" variables of linear programming attain significant import when they are interpreted as shadow prices. Second, the widespread interest in CBA has placed the term "shadow pricing" in the vocabulary of most policy analysts, independent of its linear programming heritage, as some form of cost-measurement technique.

A *shadow price* may be defined as a value associated with a unit of some good which indicates how much some specified index of performance can be increased (or decreased) by the use (or loss) of the marginal unit of that commodity. This definition applies equally to the linear programming and CBA uses of the term, suggesting that an understanding of the term in one of its uses will facilitate its appreciation in the other. (This is the tack pursued in the next chapter.) If the index of performance is social well-being, then the implications of shadow pricing for CBA are immediately clear: shadow prices are the social values of goods created, used up, or otherwise affected by a project.

4.5.1   The Use of Shadow Prices

The need for shadow prices arises with the recognition that market prices do not always accurately reflect social value. When a value other than market price is ascribed to a good in CBA,

---

[4] Subject to the qualification that the project effects are known to be minor to most impacted individuals.

then we refer to that value as a shadow price. The reader should be aware from the outset that there is no comprehensive and foolproof set of procedures for shadow pricing. Unfortunately, subjective judgment often weighs heavily in shadow-pricing exercises.

The rationale for shadow pricing is simple. Decisions must be made, and any decision implies that some valuations have been made. Setting out valuations explicitly should always be done, for it can only help clarify the issues. If market valuations are not available or are not appropriate, then explicit values must be imputed. The imputed values, if they are to improve the decision, should reflect social values. Such imputed values are shadow prices.

Nowhere are caveats more critical than with shadow pricing. This is particularly true when market prices exist, but shadow prices are considered in lieu of market prices. It is very difficult to avoid the appearance, if not the fact, of arbitrariness when adjusting market prices. Often, the credibility of the analysis (hence, its value as a decision aid) is better served by using market prices as the basis for calculations, but carefully noting the direction and likely magnitude of their bias. Thus, a market price may serve as a boundary value when a divergence between price and social value exists.

Determining shadow prices is not costless; rather, very significant costs may easily be incurred in gathering and processing enough information to construct *good* shadow prices. Indeed, a judgment must always be made as to whether the benefits of constructing a shadow price—in terms of a better decision—are worth the cost involved. *An* estimate can always be made; however, obtaining *good* estimates can be quite difficult.

Efforts to circumvent the need for shadow prices are usually worthwhile. A very common situation wherein shadow pricing appears to be necessary, but can be avoided, arises when a project involves the creation of a new good or substantial alteration of an existing good, and when that good is an output to the production of other goods. Research and development (R & D) projects are often of this type. Since the good would be new, there is no existing market from which to draw a market price.

Often it is possible to trace the impact of the new product to its ultimate impact on the consumption of goods and services by society. By relating the new good to final-consumption goods, the value of that new good can be expressable in terms of the market price of the final goods upon which its existence somehow makes impact.

An example will clarify this point. One of the authors recently conducted a CBA of new space communication technologies. The object of the analysis was to determine which of a large number of advanced-technology concepts useful to satellite communication systems should be brought, through the expenditure of R & D funds, from rough "drawing-board" designs to operational hardware items. The chief problem was in determining the value of the benefits of these hardware items, since fairly good R & D cost estimates were available. Since the products did not yet exist, there were obviously no market prices to serve as guides. Moreover, even projections of selling prices for these items were of doubtful value, since the market for many of these goods resembles a bilateral oligopoly,[5] and very little can be said about the way prices reflect social value in such circumstances. In particular, inferences about social willingness to pay may not be possible.

In addressing their technological implications, it was observed that each potential hardware development effectively allowed weight savings in the satellite portion of the communication system. Weight savings per se have little value, however, because it is usually most efficient to launch the heaviest payload permitted by the launch vehicle. A lighter payload is still launched on the same vehicle since only discrete-sized vehicles are available. A lighter payload only saves fuel, a negligible cost when compared with the total launch cost. Weight savings, however, do permit additional communication capacity to be carried on the satellite of given (maximum) weight. With each

---

[5] A *bilateral oligopoly* is a market in which there are very few buyers and very few sellers of the products being traded. Prices depend on many factors, including the bargaining power of each firm as well as sundry strategic considerations.

satellite now capable of handling a large communication load, fewer satellites are needed to provide the requisite capacity. The ultimate effect, then, is that the advanced-technology items may be valued in terms of the number of launches that may be avoided. A typical launch costs in the neighborhood of $25 M. In this example, shadow pricing was avoided by tracing the effects of the project to an ultimate effect on social consumption possibilities. Assuming (as is reasonable) that the resources used in satellite launchings have alternative values, then a saved launch makes approximately $25 M in resources available to the economy for other uses.

4.5.2   Shadow Prices and Linear Programming

To clearly appreciate shadow pricing, it is useful to view the concept within the context of a linear program. Let us imagine a simple economy whose main features are as follows:

(A)   There are two types of goods, final-consumption goods and raw materials. Call these X and Y, respectively.

(B)   The members of society have valued the final goods by attaching prices to them. The higher the price, the more valuable that good is to each individual. These prices are P_i $(i = 1, 2, \ldots, N)$.

(C)   There is a linear technology through which society transforms the raw materials into final consumption goods:

$$X_1 = a_{11}Y_{11} + a_{21}Y_{21} + \cdots + a_{M1}Y_{M1},$$
$$X_2 = a_{12}Y_{12} + a_{22}Y_{22} + \cdots + a_{M2}Y_{M2},$$
$$\vdots$$
$$X_N = a_{1N}Y_{1N} + a_{2N}Y_{2N} + \cdots + a_{MN}Y_{MN};$$

X_i is the number of units of consumption good i produced, and i goes from 1 through N. Y_{ij} is the number of units of raw material i used in the production of final good j. The a_{ij} are nonnegative parameters.

(D) The total amount of any raw material available for use in any time period is limited. The maximum available amounts are $\bar{Y}_j$ ($j = 1, 2, \ldots, M$). Thus, society's production process must also satisfy

$$Y_{11} + Y_{12} + \cdots + Y_{1N} \leq \bar{Y}_1,$$

$$Y_{21} + Y_{22} + \cdots + Y_{2N} \leq \bar{Y}_2,$$

$$\vdots$$

$$Y_{M1} + Y_{M2} + \cdots + Y_{MN} \leq \bar{Y}_M.$$

(E) Society's goal is to maximize the value of its total production. That is, of all feasible sets of final goods $(X_1, X_2, \ldots, X_N)$, society wants to produce that set which maximizes

$$V = P_1 X_1 + P_2 X_2 + \cdots + P_N X_N.$$

When society's production-planning agency solves the problem stated in Assumption E, it finds that it has incidentally found values for the linear programming dual variables λ_1, $\lambda_2, \ldots, \lambda_M$. Dual variable λ_j corresponds to the constraint on $\bar{Y}_j$ in D. These λ's would not be very interesting except for the remarkable fact that, if society were somehow able to find one more unit of Y_j to use in production, the value of the final output would increase by λ_j. That is, λ_j tells the production-planning agency how much the marginal unit of Y_j is worth to society. Briefly,

$$\lambda_j = \frac{\partial V}{\partial Y_j}.$$

Needless to say, the λ_j are the shadow prices of the Y_j.

Now let us consider the performance of CBA in this simple economy. Two projects have been identified as possibly worth undertaking. Each involves a new method of "extracting" raw materials from the earth. Because of political considerations, only one project can be chosen for implementation (a maximum of one, that is, since neither may actually be worthwhile). Project Alpha would involve taking one unit of Y_1 and two units of Y_2 out of the production of final goods, but would use them to increase the extraction of Y_3 by two units. The new Y_3 then could be used in the production of consumer goods. Project Beta would use one Y_1 and one Y_3 to get three more Y_2. Suppose that the shadow prices of Y_1, Y_2, and Y_3 are 1, 2, and 3 respectively.

How can we evaluate these projects? By Assumption E, society is interested only in the output of final consumer goods—the X's. Society's interest in raw materials extends only to how they affect production; raw materials have no social value in themselves. Thus, the appropriate way to attack this problem is to ask how Projects Alpha and Beta would affect V, the value of final output. Clearly it would be useful to have some way to relate changes in the Y's to V. But this is precisely the role of the shadow price! The cost–benefit analysis of Alpha and Beta must be performed in terms of the relevant shadow prices. Table 4.1 summarizes the analyses. Project Beta turns out to be the preferred alternative, since it would increase V by 2, whereas Alpha would only increase V by 1. Cost–benefit analysis is a trivial task in this simple economy.

A final crucial point remains to be made in the context of this model. Suppose that the Y's had prices associated with them—prices that, for some reason, did not correspond in direct proportion to the shadow prices, the λ's. Then, however tempting, it would be incorrect to use those prices in CBA. They would be completely irrelevant to the problem. *Only if there were some systematic deviation of those prices from the shadow prices would the former be useful in inferring the values of the latter.* This, as we shall see, constitutes the foundation of actual attempts to derive shadow prices, which will be covered later.

TABLE 4.1
Calculation of Benefits and Costs in Hypothetical Example

Project	Social benefit	Social cost
Alpha	$2Y_3 \times 3 = 6$	$1Y_1 \times 1 + 2Y_2 \times 2 = 5$
Beta	$3Y_2 \times 2 = 6$	$1Y_1 \times 1 + 1Y_3 \times 3 = 4$

4.5.3 Shadow Prices and Economic Theory

A linear-programming approach to determining shadow prices for an actual economy might seem a good way to proceed. The foregoing model, after all, does capture many of the salient aspects of reality: consumption goods and raw materials (physical resources, capital, labor), a determinate technology that transforms one into the other, an objective of maximizing the value of production, limited resources, etc. Why can we not just construct the actual problem, solve it, and thereby determine the dual variables, or shadow prices? One reason is simply that an actual economy is far too complex for a good, sufficiently detailed model to be constructed. In addition to inherent nonlinearities and even nonconvexities (which are major obstacles to analysis), there would be many thousands of technical relationships to be estimated, and hundreds of institutional and other noneconomic types of constraints. However, the primary reason is that there is a far better method than this—better in the sense that the expected accuracy of the modeling approach can be achieved at much less cost. This method is economic theory.

The theme which has attracted the most attention from modern economists is construction and analysis of the model of a perfectly competitive economy. This model is based on the following assumptions:

(A)   In the market for each good, there are a large number of relatively small buyers and sellers.

(B)   All firms in the same industry produce similar goods. Thus, no buyer has any a priori reason to prefer the output of one firm over that of another. Another way of saying the same thing is that products are completely standardized among firms, and there is no brand loyalty among consumers.

(C)   Resources are completely mobile. Owners of productive resources (land, labor, capital) are free to put them to whatever use they please. People can work in, or sell their physical resources to, any industry they please. There are no barriers to establishing a firm in any industry.

(D)   Each economic agent is an optimizer. Each individual acts to maximize his satisfaction, each firm acts to maximize its profits.

(E)   Each economic agent has perfect knowledge. He knows, with certainty, all present and future prices.

(F)   There are no price rigidities. Prices may move up or down subject to market pressures.

If the above conditions hold, it is easy to prove that:

(1)   prices are determined by the market equilibration of supply and demand; and

(2)   in the long run, all goods are produced and sold at the lowest possible price.

If some additional conditions hold, then another result very useful to CBA can be established. Among these conditions are:

(G)   Individuals are "selfish." Each person's feelings of well-being are determined exclusively by his own consumption. He is free of both sympathy and envy in the sense that the misfortunes and fortunes of others do not affect his feeling of satisfaction.

(H)   Individuals are "greedy." More is better. A person never reaches the satiation point. He always feels better off by consuming more.

(I)   Individual preferences are such that the rate at which additional amounts of one good may be substituted for another diminishes. That is, in the language of the economists, diminishing marginal rates of substitution between goods exist and indifference curves are convex to the origin.

(J)   There are no production processes that exhibit increasing returns to scale.

(K)   There are no externalities.

(L)   There are no public goods.

(M)   There is no government taxation (except, perhaps, a head or poll tax) and no government subsidizations of any good.

(N)   All goods are exchanged in markets.

(O)   All markets are in equilibrium.

If Conditions A–O are satisfied, then economic theory has established this very important result: *all goods have market prices, and the market prices are exactly equal to the corresponding shadow prices* (true social values).

Once again, use of CBA would reduce to a relatively trivial matter. This time, however, we did not have to resort to a programming model of the economy. Instead, by employing the results of economic theory, we have arrived at the same point—an environment in which foolproof CBA can be accomplished.

But what form of chicanery is this? The conditions of this model are as unrealistic as the construction of the programming model was impossible. It appears that we have not gained much at all. Or have we? The key is *systematic deviation*. Even though Conditions A–O may not hold, through economic theory we can often predict, by determining which assumptions are violated, the direction in which the observed price deviates from the shadow price. Sometimes, but less often, it is possible to make a reasonably good estimate of the magnitude of the deviation. When prices do not exist, that is, when there are no markets for the goods (like public parks), through economic theory we can at least suggest the principles and problems of measurement to guide the analyst in making his approximations.

This, then, is the forte of attacking shadow pricing with economic theory rather than mathematical programming. While neither can be directly applied to reality, the former takes account of the systematic deviations of reality from the idealized model, whereas the latter cannot. But make no mistake, economic theory is far from a panacea. A great deal of information is needed to determine shadow prices, information that is often not readily available. However, even this quantity of information does not approach the amount required for the construction of a full-scale model of the economy—a model from which meaningful dual variables could be elicited.

To illustrate the use of economic theory in deriving shadow prices through the analysis of systematic deviations from the ideal model (Assumptions A–O), consider the case of a hypothetical producer of newsprint, who occupies a monopolistic position in his market. Externalities are involved in both the production and sales ends of operations. The production of newsprint pollutes the water source, causing an external diseconomy. The final product, the newsprint, provides an external benefit (economy) to society by virtue of its role as a medium for distributing vast amounts of information. Such information flows are the foundation of political democracy (informing readers about issues, world events, government actions) and economic competition (advertisements about new products, prices, new stores, and the like). Presumably, the value of newsprint to society exceeds its relatively low final cost to consumers. For example, an individual may be willing to pay $50 per year for a given quantity (and quality) of printed news, but society may feel that the overall value of keeping a citizen well informed is $55 or $60, or even more.

Suppose that a government policy is being considered, which will have the effect of increasing newsprint production by some marginal amount, perhaps through more favorable tax treatment. How does shadow pricing apply to this cost–benefit decision?

Before answering this question, let us consider the economics of the "ideal" firm. This will provide a base for the systematic deviations of the newsprint firm from ideal characteristics. Among other things, the ideal firm is a price taker (meaning that its relatively small size forces the firm to accept the prevailing market price as the price at which its output will be sold) and does not induce any external economies or diseconomies. Note, then, that our hypothetical newsprint firm is in violation of Assumptions A and K above. Figure 4.2 presents the salient features of the ideal firm. The market price is OB. Since the firm feels it can sell all it wishes at OB, the demand curve it faces is

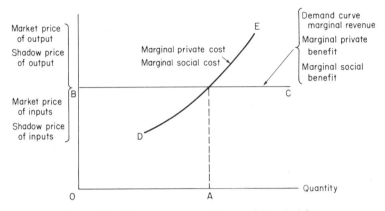

Figure 4.2   Salient economic features of the ideal firm.

BC. The constant selling price means that *BC* is the marginal revenue curve, showing the additional revenue derived from an additional unit of output. Since demand reflects willingness to pay, which is the measure of benefits, *BC* is also the marginal private benefit curve, and since there are no externalities, *BC* is the marginal social benefit curve as well. *DE* represents the marginal cost of production for the firm. Because there are no externalities, *DE* is also the marginal social cost of production. Assuming it maximizes profit, the firm's output is *OA.* Thus, with respect to marginal changes in output, *OB* is simultaneously the market price of the output, the shadow price of output (true value to consumers), the market price of inputs and the shadow price of inputs (true measure of the cost to society of using those inputs). Since *OB* is directly observable, CBA is a simple matter. To reiterate the point made earlier, the calculation of gains and losses is an almost trivial matter in the "ideal" economy.

Turning now to the economics of the newsprint firm, the situation becomes more complex as we consider how it deviates from that of the ideal firm. As a monopolist, it faces the entire market demand for its output. Such a demand, of course, is downward sloping to the right—only at lower prices can more be sold. The demand curve, identical to the marginal private benefits curve, is *AB* in Figure 4.3. Since there are external economies

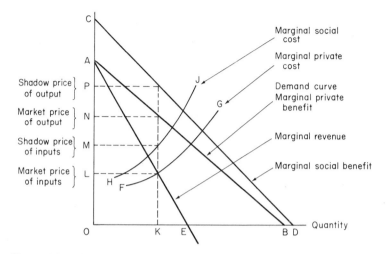

Figure 4.3 Salient economic features of the hypothetical "newsprint" firm.

associated with newsprint production, the marginal social benefit curve lies somewhere above *AB*, say at *CD*. The firm will
produce *OK* units of output, since marginal revenue just equals
the firm's marginal cost at that output level. Then, with respect to
marginal changes in output, *OL* is the firm's unit production
cost, *OM* is the unit poduction cost to society (*OM* > *OL* because
of the pollution by-product of the production process), *ON* is the
price that the firm will charge per unit, and *OP* is the value to
society of each unit. Now note that only *ON* is directly observable. *OL* may usually be estimated reasonably well by using
accounting data and knowledge of the firm's production operations. But for CBA, *OM* and *OP* are the crucial magnitudes. In
contrast to the case of the ideal model, these CBA-relevant
magnitudes are not directly observable. However, and here is the
solid contribution of economic theory, the requisite information
is now neatly circumscribed. What is needed is the local (in the
neighborhood *K*) properties of *HJ* and *CD*. Had we gone to a
programming model, far more information would have been
necessary.

4.6 SUMMARY

In summary, we have shown that shadow prices can be thought of either as dual variables arising from mathematical programming or as true economic valuations. In principle, the two meanings are identical. Why? Because, while the programming approach *explicitly* optimizes over a set of constraints, the results of economic theory have *implicitly* accounted for the same optimizing behavior. The market demand curve, for example, is based on consumer utility maximization. In economic theory each economic agent (consumer or firm) is viewed as an optimizer. The equilibrium conditions in economics are nothing more than first- and second-order optimization conditions. In a sense, this is nothing more than Adam Smith's notorious "invisible hand." Relying on economic theory rather than programming for shadow-pricing guidance exploits what order there is in economic behavior. In a sense, the programming approach forces one to reestablish already well-known results, and to collect excess data. In deriving shadow prices, then, the main contribution of economic theory is the specification of the minimum requisite information, accomplished by exploiting the systematic deviations of the real world from the "ideal" competitive model.

5

SHADOW PRICING

"No data yet," he answered. "It is a capital mistake to theorize before you have all the evidence. It biases the judgement."

Sherlock Holmes to Watson. Sir Arthur Conan Doyle, *A Study in Scarlet*

5.1 INTRODUCTION

In the previous chapter we discussed the overall approach to quantification adopted in CBA. Starting with the postulate that social value is measured by willingness to pay, we showed that market prices can reflect willingness to pay, and that in a perfectly competitive economy market prices can reflect social cost as well. We showed that an efficient way to approach the calculation of shadow prices, in real situations deviating from the perfectly competitive ideal, is to attempt to take account of the manner and extent to which the deviations occur.

In this chapter we treat generic situations in which the question of shadow pricing arises. These situations fall into three classes: market prices exist and reflect social value, market prices exist but are biased, and market prices do not exist.

Reiteration here of an earlier caveat is appropriate. In cost-benefit studies, shadow pricing is a task not to be undertaken lightly. At best, shadow prices are difficult to justify and often give the appearance of arbitrariness. While many (but not all!) of the theoretical issues in shadow pricing are clear-cut, the typically overwhelming problem is a lack of data to serve as the basis for estimation procedures. Shadow pricing is, in most cases, best considered to be an approach of last resort. Especially when market prices exist, it is often best to use those prices as the basis for actual calculations, relying on the principles of shadow pricing to suggest the probable direction and extent of the bias in those prices and in the final results.

5.2 MARKET PRICES EXIST AND REFLECT SOCIAL VALUE

When market prices exist and reflect social value, there is patently no need for shadow prices. This section reviews a class of circumstances in which shadow-price calculations may at first appear necessary, but, upon reflection, prove unneeded. Specifically, this situation arises when the good in question is produced and sold (to final consumers) in an imperfectly competitive market. That is, the producer–seller of the good has some monopoly power: He can exercise some control over the market price of his product. In the case of the pure monopolist, of course, he exercises complete control over price. In cases between pure monopoly and perfect competition (in which the number of sellers is greater than one but less than the number necessary to convert each seller to being a price taker) lesser degrees of price control maintain.

To simplify exposition, let us consider the polar case of pure monopoly. The point we shall illustrate is this:

> *If the only deviation of the situation under study from the assumptions of the perfectly competitive model is the presence of some monopoly power by the seller(s) of a final consumption good, the market price of the good is the social value of the marginal units of that good.*

The argument supporting this statement resembles that of Section 4.3, and is suggested by Figure 5.1. Suppose that the price charged by the seller(s) is P_1, and Q_1 units are sold. The willingness to pay of consumers for the last few units is clearly P_1. Otherwise, more or less than Q_1 would have been purchased at P_1. By Postulates I and II of Section 4.2, the social value of the marginal units of Q is P_1 when Q_1 units are purchased. Now note that the argument is completely general with respect to the price being charged by the seller(s). Indeed, if the price were P_2 and Q_2 units were sold, the value of the marginal units of Q would be P_2. In the latter case, because fewer units are available, their social value is greater at the margin.

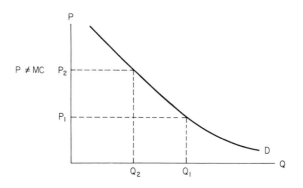

Figure 5.1   Demand faced by a monopolistic seller.

5.3 MARKET PRICES EXIST BUT ARE BIASED

In this section we consider a number of common situations in which market prices exist, but are under- or overestimates of social values. As mentioned earlier, the probable existence of a bias is itself not usually a sufficient reason to undertake construction of shadow prices. Rather, the direction and likely magnitude of the bias should be reflected in a sensitivity analysis and in the construction of upper and lower bounds on the estimate. In any case, the cost–benefit analyst should always search out and remain aware of biases in the relevant market prices.

5.3.1 Effects on Inputs to Monopolistic Markets

As discussed in Section 5.2, market prices are reflections of the social values of final goods produced under monopolistic conditions. However, the market prices of the inputs used by monopolistic producers understate the social values of those inputs because the monopolistic producer "marks up" the inputs as they are transformed by the production process and sold to final consumers. Since the "markup" forms part of the final price (that consumers are willing to pay), it is part of the social value of the final good. Since the price of an input does not include the "markup," its price understates its social value.

For example, consider the social value of coal used in electricity generation. Electricity is produced by regulated monopolies in a declining-average-cost industry. The price of electricity is set above the marginal cost of electricity production. Suppose that a unit of coal costs $C, and the use of that unit increases electricity production by one unit, which is sold at a price of $P. Since the utility sets price above marginal cost, the cost of the coal $C must be less than $P, the price of the electricity produced by the coal. Now what is the social value of that unit of coal? Is it $C, the price of coal? Or is it $P, the price of the electricity it produced? The answer is $P, for if that unit of coal were not available, society would forego consumption (of electricity) valued at $\$P$. Thus, the price of the good understates its value.

The general line of reasoning is illustrated in Figure 5.2. Assume that X is the only input in the production of Q, which is produced under monopolistic conditions. The price of X is market determined and is not affected by the producer(s) of Q. Assume that one unit of X is used to produce one unit of Q. The upper diagram of Figure 5.2 shows the market for X in which its price is determined by the forces of supply and demand. Since X is the sole input to Q, the price of X is the marginal cost of producing a unit of Q. The producer of Q, assumed to be a profit

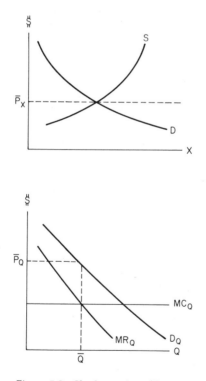

Figure 5.2   Shadow price of inputs.

maximizer, produces a number of Q so that the marginal cost of production just equals marginal revenue. Thus, $\bar{Q}$ units are produced, and they are sold at a price of $\bar{P}_Q$ each. What is the social value of the last unit of X used in the production of Q? Clearly, it is P_Q and not P_X. The reader may wish to convince himself that the more competitive the Q industry, and hence the more elastic the demand faced by each producer, the less the divergence between the price of X and its social value. This result is intuitively appealing since the more competitive industry will have a smaller "markup" of price over marginal cost. Also, as suggested by Figure 5.2, it is the excess of price over marginal cost of Q that accounts for the divergence between the price and social value of X.[1]

[1] Mathematically, this point can be seen as follows. Let $Q = F(X)$ be the production function, and suppose that Q is produced by a monopolist, and the only use for X is in the production of Q. The demand for X is derived from the demand for Q, and is such that the price of X, P_X, must equal the marginal revenue product of X in the production of Q, or MRP_{XQ}. Thus

$$P_X = MRP_{XQ}.$$

It is well known that MRP_{XQ} is the marginal revenue from Q times marginal product of X in the production of Q, or

$$MRP_{XQ} = MR_Q \times MP_{XQ}.$$

The social value of a unit of Q, $S(Q)$, as argued in Section 5.2, is simply the market price of Q, P_Q. The social value of X, since its only use is in the production of Q, rests in its contribution to that production. Thus,

$$S(X) = \frac{dS(Q)}{dX} = \frac{dS(Q)}{dQ}\frac{dQ}{dX} = P_Q\frac{dQ}{dX} = P_Q MP_{XQ}.$$

Now, the difference between the social value of X and the price of X, can be expressed as

$$S(X) - P_X = P_Q MP_{XQ} - MR_Q MP_{XQ} = (P_Q - MR_Q)MP_{XQ}.$$

Since we assume that the producer of Q is a profit maximizer, the marginal revenue from Q must be equal to marginal cost of Q, or $MR_Q = MC_Q$. Finally, we have

$$S(X) - P_X = (P_Q - MC_Q)MP_{XQ}.$$

That is, the excess of price over marginal cost of Q accounts for the discrepancy between the social value and price of X. If $P_Q = MC_Q$, as would occur in a competitive equilibrium, then $S(X) = P_X$.

5.3.2 Unemployment of Resources

Economists refer to the *factors of production*—labor, capital, and land—as the resources of the economy. The more restrictive notions of such resources as minerals, oil deposits, and timber stands are subsumed in the classification *land*. Whenever any of these factors are available but not being used to the fullest possible extent, we say that *resource unemployment* exists. *Capital* means tools, machines, and other manufactured means of production.

In a perfectly functioning competitive market economy, unemployment of any resource is a strictly temporary phenomenon. Here *unemployment* simply means that at the current market price, the quantity supplied exceeds the quantity demanded. Market forces then will tend to lower the market price (which increases quantity demanded and/or decreases quantity supplied) until a full employment market equilibrium is achieved. If the quantity supplied always exceeds the quantity demanded, the price falls to zero. Such is the case for the good, air.

It is clear that ours is not a perfectly functioning competitive-market economy. This is especially true in the labor market, since unemployment does not drive the price of the good (wages are the price of labor) down.[2] Thus, unemployment can be more than strictly temporary. When price does not respond to supply and demand, and consequently does not reflect social values (since the existing price-quantity point will not be on the demand curve), market price is a biased measure in CBA. We now examine each factor category to see how unemployment affects CBA measurements.

LABOR

Labor that would *otherwise* be unemployed should be valued at a zero social cost when employed in project—in spite of the

---

[2] This is usually attributed to the presence of labor unions, which can be considered to have a monopoly of labor. This is a key facet in Keynesian macroeconomics, in which the theory asserts the likelihood of an unemployment equilibrium.

fact that labor has a dollar cost. To see why this rule is valid, let us illustrate its derivation. Recall that a project can be viewed as moving society from one state to another. In the initial state S^0 there is one unemployed worker A who is receiving $50 per week in unemployment compensation. For simplicity, suppose that taxpayer B alone is taxed $50 to pay A. The new state S' has A employed by the government, earning $150 per week, and B's taxes are increased to cover this new government expenditure. Assume that A's output has a social value of $150 per week. Table 5.1 summarizes the social accounting (on a weekly basis). The government's unemployment payments to A, and B's tax payments to the government are *transfer* payments. Transfer payments do not reflect the production of goods or services.

Note, first, that net social value in S^0 must be zero if S^0 is to be the base of reference. The change from S^0 to S' entails a change in social costs of $100 = $150 − $50. The corresponding change in social benefits is $250 = $150 + $150 − $50. Therefore, the net social value of the change from S^0 to S' equals the change in benefits less the change in costs, or

net social value $(S^0$ to $S') = $150 = $250 − $100.

Once such an exercise has been performed, its simpler *equivalent* may be employed, and that is the rule stated above. To reiterate, the rule states that A's employment costs society nothing if A would be otherwise employed. Of course, the social

TABLE 5.1
Accounting For Labor Employment

State	Cost		Benefits	
S^0	$50	(value of consumption foregone by B)	$50	(value of consumption enjoyed by A)
S'	$150	(value of consumption foregone by B)	$150	(value of consumption enjoyed by A)
			$150	(value to society of A's production)

benefit is the value of A's production. The shorthand accounting procedure implied by the rule is presented in Table 5.1. Of course, the net social value of S^0 to S' again equals $150. Ordinarily, the marginal social benefit resulting from A's employment would not be easily isolated. Rather, that benefit would be aggregated into some broader category. A's employment cost, on the other hand, will be specifically recorded. For that reason, the rule is more concerned with the cost of employment rather than benefit.

Properly interpreted, the rule means that we must be very wary of counting jobs created as a benefit of a project, for this is correct *only* if the job holders would be otherwise unemployed. Two pitfalls must be avoided. First, a job created by a project will exist over a number of years. Costs and benefits must be tallied for each year of the project. Even if the job goes to an unemployed individual in the first year of the project, there is no reason to suppose that this individual would remain unemployed over the time span during which the job exists. Unemployment is cylical. The proper approach, assuming that there is current unemployment, would be to value the social cost of employment at zero for the first several years and then at the wage rate thereafter.

The second pitfall is for the analyst to suppose that his is the truly marginal project. It is tempting to look at unemployment statistics and, noting that there is *always* some unemployment (even beyond frictional unemployment, or people between jobs), conclude that this project will draw from that unemployed labor pool. The difficulty is that, if this approach is taken in each project, the "margin" may well become 10 million workers wide. Again, the proper approach is to value labor costs at the wage rate, except when the analyst is reasonably sure that the jobs *will* be filled by the unemployed. Such certainty, given the current state of economic forecasting, cannot extend beyond several years for the general labor market. However, for certain classes of jobs, it may be possible to construct an employment probability distribution over future years. This approach, if warranted within the context of the analysis, could provide the decision maker with a better grade of information.

CAPITAL

Capital that would be *otherwise* unemployed should be valued at zero social cost when employed in a project. The original or replacement costs, or the depreciated value, are simply not relevant. Society incurs the cost of producing capital when it is produced, for the social cost is the consumption opportunities currently precluded by devoting resources to capital construction instead of consumer goods. Only present and future costs are relevant to decisions; past (sunk) costs are not. For example, if rotors to capture wind energy could be placed on unmodified electric transmission towers, the social cost of using those towers for the project would be zero. Their construction costs were incurred in the past—their social cost has already been paid. However, if the same project requires new towers, their construction *is* a social cost of the project.

LAND

Land that would be otherwise unemployed should be valued at zero social cost when employed in a project. Land is a good that provides a time flow of service. The price of a tract of land is usefully considered to be an approximation of the net present value of the flow of rental receipts. (This would be exactly true in a land market characterized by the perfect knowledge of future land uses and demands.) This viewpoint explains why idle land is valuable. The higher the price of a tract, the higher are the anticipated rental receipts. Thus, the market price of a tract is a good measure of its social value because rental receipts are based on the productive capacity of the tract. When a tract is employed in a project to the exclusion of other uses and for a significant length of time, the market price should be taken to be the social cost of the land. For shorter periods, a rental value should be taken to be social cost. If the analyst can be reasonably certain that the land would remain idle for some years, zero social cost should be charged for those years.

5.3.3 Nonmarginal Price Changes

CONSUMERS' SURPLUS

Up to this point we have restricted our attention to situations in which the production of goods has increased or decreased without a concomitant change in the price of the good. Then, social benefit or cost is measured by the price multiplied by the change in quantity. Since we admit that reasonable approximations are the best that we can hope to achieve with CBA, even a small (marginal) price change need not alter this approach. Then it may make little difference to the final result whether the change in quantity is multiplied by the new price or by the old price.

However, when there is a substantial (nonmarginal) change in price, greater precision is demanded. It is achieved through the use of the concept of consumers' surplus. In Figure 5.3, let AD represent a consumers' demand for Q, and let the price of Q be P^0. The demand curve shows that if the price of Q were 50, the consumer would purchase one unit. In other words, the consumer's willingness to pay (WTP) for the first unit of Q is 50. However, since the price is P^0, the consumer pays only P^0 for that unit. Thus, the consumer receives a net benefit, or surplus, from that first unit of $50 - P^0$. Likewise, we could argue that the surplus on the second unit is $48 - P^0$, on the third unit it is $46 - P^0$, and so on. The consumer's surplus on the last unit purchased, the fifteenth in the figure, is zero. How much is the consumer's total surplus from consuming 15 units? Clearly a very good approximation is the area ABP^0. Here, ABP^0 is the net benefit from the consumption of 15 units of Q, since the consumer's total WTP for those units is the area ABQ^0O, his or her cost is P^0BQ^0O, and

$$ABP^0 = ABQ^0O - P^0BQ^0O.$$

Now suppose that a project has the effect of lowering the price of Q to P', resulting in an increase in consumption from Q^0 to Q'. The net benefit to the consumer of this change in status

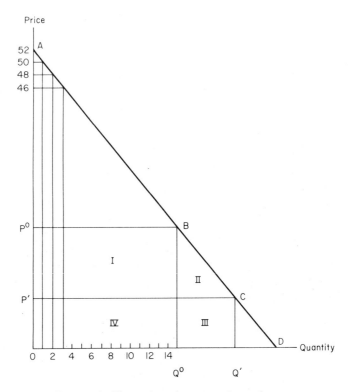

Figure 5.3   Illustration of consumer's surplus.

(from S^0 characterized by P^0 and Q^0 to S' characterized by P' and Q') must be equal to the increase in WTP less the increase in expenditure.

In S^0,

$$\text{WTP} = ABQ^0O.$$

In S',

$$\text{WTP} = ACQ'O.$$

$$\Delta\text{WTP}(S^0 \text{ to } S') = ACQ'O - ABQ^0O.$$

$$= BCQ'Q^0,$$

or

$$\Delta WTP = II + III.$$

In S^0,

$$expenditure = P^0BQ^0O$$

$$= I + IV.$$

In S',

$$expenditure = P'CQ'O$$

$$= III + IV.$$

$$\Delta \text{ expenditure} = (III + IV) - (I + IV) = III - I.$$

Net benefit of movement S^0 to S'

$$= \Delta WTP - \Delta \text{ expenditure}$$

$$= (II + III) - (III - I)$$

$$= I + II.$$

The area $P^0BCP^1 = I + II$ is the value to the consumer of the drop in price. It is called the *consumer's surplus* because of the price change. This is the value relevant to CBA when a substantial change in price results from the implementation of a project. When the empirically estimated demand curve is linear, the calculation of net benefit simplifies to

$$(P^0 - P^1)\left(\frac{Q^0 + Q^1}{2}\right).$$

Our discussion has centered on the individual consumer's demand curve. The objection may be raised that only market demand curves are available to the analyst (and even these are usually difficult to come by!). Does the same approach still apply? Absolutely! By using a two-person model, we can illustrate the equivalence between using the consumer-surplus approach on a market demand curve and using it on individual demand curves, summing those values over the individuals. The demand curves for Consumers α and β, and the corresponding market demand curve are given in Figure 5.4. The market demand curve is the horizontal sum of the individual demand

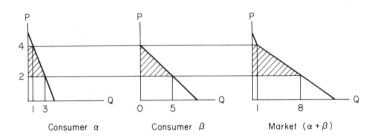

Figure 5.4   Summation of consumer's surplus.

curves. This means that at any price, the market demand curve shows the sum of the individual quantities demanded at that price. As examples, at a price of 4, the market demand curve indicates the quantity demanded is 1. This corresponds to quantities demanded 1 and 0 by Consumers α and β, respectively. At $P = 2$, the quantity demanded in the market is 8, corresponding to the quantities 3 demanded by α and 5 demanded by β. Suppose that the price is initially at 4 and drops to 2 as the result of a project. The shaded areas under α's and β's demand curves are the relevant measures of the value of that price change to these consumers. This was the conclusion drawn above. It is obvious from the construction of the market demand curve that the shaded area under that curve is in fact the sum of the other two areas. Thus, the consumer-surplus approach for an individual is directly applicable to a market.

COMPENSATING VARIATION

We have argued that the willingness to pay (WTP) value of a good to an individual for CBA and that a certain area under a demand curve can be equated with WTP. For *all practical purposes*, this equation is unassailable. However, from a strictly theoretic viewpoint, it is not quite correct. The following discussion is not meant to modify the use of consumer surplus as described above; it is intended only to elucidate a technical point that might otherwise trouble some readers.

The proper way to interpret a demand curve, such as that

illustrated in Figure 5.5 is this. When D is the demand curve for Q for a specified time interval (that is, per week, per month, per year), then, if the price is constant at P^0 for that interval, the consumer will purchase Q^0 over that interval. If the price is constant at P' for that interval, the consumer will purchase Q' for that interval. If the price is constant at P'', and so forth.

The demand curve does *not* mean: If the price is initially at P^0, the consumer will purchase Q^0. If the price drops to P' during the time interval for which the demand curve is drawn (for example, at the beginning of the second week for a monthly demand curve), the consumer will purchase an additional $Q' - Q^0$; if it drops again to P'' during the interval, he will purchase an additional $Q'' - Q', \ldots$.

While this is not a strictly correct interpretation, a little reflection will indicate it is the one on which the consumer-surplus approach is based.

To derive an exact measure of the value of a price drop to an individual, it is convenient to phrase the question this way: What is the maximum amount of money the consumer would be

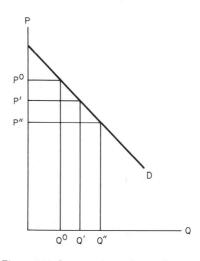

Figure 5.5   Interpreting a demand curve.

willing to pay to be able to buy (all that he wants of) the good at
the lower price rather than the higher price?

The answer to the question is that amount of money which
leaves the consumer at the same level of utility at the lower price
with less money to spend as at the high price with more money
to spend. That amount of money is called his *compensating
variation* (of income).

To determine a compensating variation, the analyst must
either know the consumer's utility function (a practical impossibility) or be able to subject him to some elaborate experiment
designed to reveal the compensating variation (very costly).

Fortunately, there are two theorems that obviate the need to
attempt a computation of compensating variation. Loosely stated,
they are:

THEOREM 1

The smaller the price change in question, the closer is the
consumer's surplus to the compensating variation.

THEOREM 2

The smaller the proportion of income spent on the good in
question, the closer is the consumer's surplus to the compensating variation.

Actually, Theorem 1 does not really help us too much, since
in practice we restrict our attention to significant price changes.
However, the second theorem is quite useful since, at least in
advanced economies such as our own, almost every good consumed, with the exception of housing, accounts for a small
proportion of total expenditures. Thus, for *practical purposes*,
consumer's surplus is a close enough measure of the value of a
price change, the technical difficulty notwithstanding.

PRODUCERS' SURPLUS

Just as consumers receive a "surplus" when they purchase
goods at a price lower than the maximum they are willing to pay,

so do producers of goods receive a surplus when they sell goods at a price higher than the least they are willing to accept for those goods. This surplus reaped by sellers is known as *producers' surplus*.

As an illustration of the concept, consider a self-employed craftsman who builds and sells grandfather clocks. Because of competition in the market, he can sell his clocks for no more than $450 apiece. His only production costs are materials and labor. The materials for each clock cost the craftsman $250. It takes 20 hr of labor to produce one grandfather clock. On a monthly basis, he values the first 160 hr of labor time at $6 per hour, the next 20 at $8 per hour, the next 20 at $10 per hour, and so on. His increasing marginal valuation of his labor time reflects the fact that each extra hour worked results in a lost hour of leisure. As total monthly leisure time diminishes, the value of marginal leisure hours increases. Table 5.2 is a summary of the foregoing information. On each of the first eight units produced, his total unit cost (including the cost of his own time) is $370. Presumably, this is the least he would be willing to accept to produce and sell each unit. However, he receives $450 in revenue on each sale. He gains a surplus of $80 on each of these first eight units. On the ninth unit, because his labor time is more costly, his surplus is $40. On the tenth unit, the producer's surplus is 0. His total producer's surplus is, of course, the sum of the surplus associated with each unit sold. Graphically, this sum is the area between his supply curve (marginal cost curve) and the price.

TABLE 5.2
Producers' Surplus Illustration

Units	Materials cost	Labor cost	Revenue	Surplus
1	250	120	450	80
⋮	⋮	⋮	⋮	⋮
8	250	120	450	80
9	250	160	450	40
10	250	200	450	0
11	250	240	450	−40

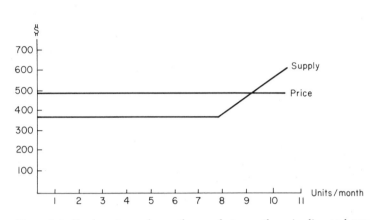

Figure 5.6   Producer's surplus as the area between the price line and supply
curve.

This is illustrated in Figure 5.6. Note that the producer's surplus
is in addition to any consumer's surplus that the purchaser of a
grandfather clock may enjoy.

5.3.4   Increasing Returns to Scale

We know that, in an "ideal" perfectly competitive economy,
firms set their prices equal to their marginal costs. Thus, market
price is a measure of both willingness to pay for the good and the
social opportunity cost (or shadow price) of that good. When a
firm's production is characterized by increasing returns to scale
(alternatively, diminishing average cost), the firm will actually
lose money—make negative profits—if its prices are set equal to
its marginal cost of production. Naturally, the firm will not
accept negative profits, and its prices will be set in excess of
marginal cost, as is done in the imperfectly competitive firm.
Thus, the market price may differ from the shadow price.

Increasing returns characterize many public utilities, and
this is the basis for the importance of this case. Public utilities
are *regulated* by government agencies. Such regulation is designed, at least in theory, to protect the consuming public against

indiscriminately high prices (excess profits) and insufficient quantities supplied. The formula that accomplishes both of these goals is average-cost pricing. This is illustrated in Figure 5.7. Here D, AC, and MC represent the market demand, average cost, and marginal cost curves, respectively. A policy of marginal-cost pricing would imply a price of OC (at which MC crosses D). However, at a price of OC and production of OG (which equates the quantity supplied to the quantity demanded at price OC), the firm's total revenue (price times quantity) is $CFGO$. The firm's total cost (average cost times quantity) is $BEGO$. The firm's loss is therefore $BEFC$. On the other hand, pricing at OA and producing OH simultaneously satisfies all demand (at that price) and covers all costs without economic profits. This is the type of outcome regulatory commissions seek to achieve.

Relevant to CBA is the fact that the social benefit of a marginal unit of output is equal to the WTP, or OA, whereas the social cost (assuming competition elsewhere in the economy) is HJ.

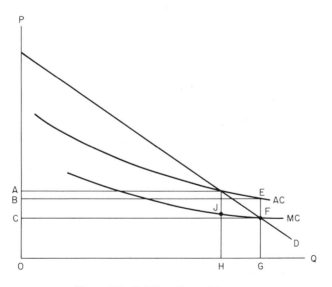

Figure 5.7 Public utility pricing.

5.3.5 Government Taxation and Subsidization

These fiscal tools of government cause observed prices to deviate from the corresponding shadow prices. While taxes and subsidies ought to be included in the price when computing WTP for the marginal unit, they should be excluded when computing the cost of producing the marginal unit. The supply and demand for good Q in a perfectly competitive economy is shown in Figure 5.8. Government levies a per unit tax on Q in the amount of t. The tax is collected from the manufacturers. This shifts the original supply curve S^0 upward t units to S'. The new equilibrium price and quantity are P' and Q'. Since, at the margin, consumers are willing to pay P' for Q', P' is the social benefit of increased output. However, C is the social cost of producing the additional units. This can be inferred from the supply curve because no economic profits are being made by the firms. All receipts are used to cover the tax and the costs of production. A government subsidy for Q may be analyzed analogously.

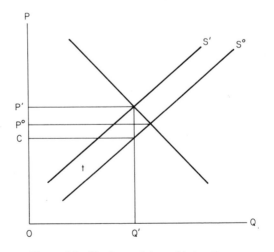

Figure 5.8   Shadow pricing with taxation.

5.3.6 Price Controls

Perhaps the best example of a situation in which the market price is a poor mirror of social value is when price controls prevail. Here, the government imposes a ceiling price or a floor price. The former allows the price to go no higher than a specified level; the latter allows it to go no lower. In both cases, the action is meant to thwart the workings of supply and demand in the market. Sometimes the thwarted market is highly competitive, for example, when price floors are levied in agricultural markets; sometimes the thwarted market is monopolistic, for example, when wage controls restrict union (monopolistic labor supplies) wage demands, or when price controls restrict prices for steel or automobiles. The effect of price controls is to move the price–quantity combination off the market demand curve. Since the demand, embodying consumer willingness to pay, reflects social value, points off the demand curve are biased indicators of social value.

Figure 5.9 is a diagrammatic representation of the price-ceiling case. If the market were free to function, the equilibrium price would be P_E and the quantity produced and sold would be Q_E. However, we assume the existence of a price ceiling P_C: the

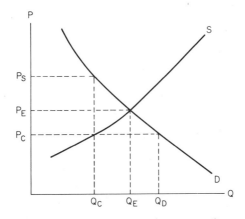

Figure 5.9 Shadow pricing with a price ceiling.

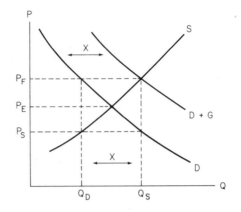

Figure 5.10   Shadow pricing with a price floor.

price charged may not exceed P_C. At P_C, suppliers are willing to produce only Q_C but consumers wish to purchase Q_D. $Q_D - Q_C$ will be desired but unavailable. According to the demand curve D the willingness to pay for the marginal units of Q when Q_C units are produced is P_S. The established price P_C understates social value by $P_S - P_C$.

Figure 5.10 is an illustration of the analysis of a price floor. The floor is set at P_F, above the equilibrium price of P_E, as determined by the intersection of S and D. At P_F, consumers wish to purchase Q_D, while suppliers will produce Q_S. However, an excess production of X amounting to $(Q_S - Q_D)$ would motivate suppliers to cut prices. In order to maintain the price floor, government must enter the market and buy[3] X units of Q. Effectively, this shifts the market demand from D to $D + G$, where $D + G$ is X units to the right of D. Thus, at P_F, consumers purchase Q_D and the government purchases X. The total demand is now sufficient to support the price P_F. What is the social value of the marginal units of Q? It depends on the disposition of those units. If they are made available to consumers, the value is

---

[3] Assume that the government effectively removes the X units from the market; for example, it could export its purchases as aid to underdeveloped countries.

clearly P_F. If they are purchased by government, they have no value to consumers. The price floor overstates the social value of output by the full price in the latter case and not at all in the former.

5.4 MARKET PRICES DO NOT EXIST

The most dire need for shadow pricing occurs when the goods or services to be valued are not exchanged on a market. The existence of market prices, at the least, gives a clue as to neighborhoods of the social values being sought. Market prices fail to exist in two important situations: externalities and public goods.

5.4.1 External Effects

External effects (or externalities or spillovers) are often, although not necessarily, identified with some form of pollution. Such effects may be said to exist when the actions of one economic agent affect the welfare of another, and the former is neither compensated (in the case of a good spillover) nor charged a fee (in the case of bad spillover) by the latter. A bad (or negative) externality either reduces utility or increases production costs, depending on whether it has impact on a consumer or a firm. In either case, the externality has a social cost. Therefore, externalities must be valued and incorporated into CBA. Public projects can give rise to external effects in two ways: through inputs to the project and through the outputs of the project.

EXTERNAL EFFECTS FROM INPUTS

Suppose that good Q is an input to a public project, $\bar{Q}$ units of Q will be used by the project, and each unit of Q produced has an external cost of e dollars. For concreteness, we can think of Q

as electric power from a coal-fired steam plant, in which electricity generation produces sulfur emissions. Should the project (using this electricity) be assessed a social cost of $e\bar{Q}$? Not necessarily. How much to assess the project depends on the supply conditions of Q. Put another way, it is necessary to determine how much more Q *is actually produced because of the project*. To illustrate, consider three supply situations: perfectly inelastic, perfectly elastic, and the "normal" case:

(a) With perfectly inelastic supply, the quantity supplied does not respond to price changes. For the relevant time period, it is rigidly fixed. Let D^0 be the original demand for Q, and D' the demand after the $\bar{Q}$ demanded by the project has been incorporated. In Figure 5.11 it is shown that the only effect of the increased demand is to raise the price of Q. Therefore, the $\bar{Q}$ units of Q will be purchased by the project, but the higher price will decrease others' purchase by Q of $\bar{Q}$. There is no increase in external effects resulting from the project. No externality charge should be levied against the project in this case.

(b) When the supply is perfectly elastic, the increase in quantity supplied exactly matches the increased quantity demanded. This is the case in which the project does subject society to increased externality costs of $e\bar{Q}$.

(c) In the normal case, where S is neither vertical nor horizontal, the increased demand causes both a price rise and increase in output. While the project again gets its $\bar{Q}$ units, some of these are given up by purchasers who do not wish to pay the higher price. The remainder constitute new production. Only the externality costs attributable to the new production should be charged against the project. Clearly, for this case, the costs are between zero and $e\bar{Q}$.

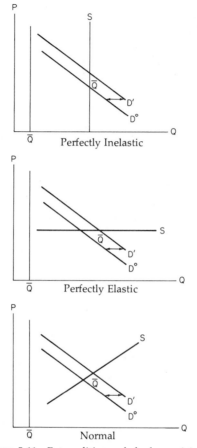

Figure 5.11 Externalities and shadow pricing.

EXTERNAL EFFECTS FROM OUTPUTS

Any external effects arising from the output of a project are to be charged against the project. For example, in the evaluation of a proposed airport, the daily aircraft noise is a cost to individuals nearby. This cost should be accounted for in the CBA.

It is often easy to determine the existence of a cost resulting from an external effect, but it is usually quite difficult to determine the magnitude of that cost because, by definition, the effects are uncompensated, or unpriced. There is no market determination of value to guide the analyst. The best approximations are necessarily quite crude. Note that the principle of value determination—willingness to pay (to avoid the externality)—still applies. The problem lies in making the principle operative. With regard to the airport noise problem, for example, one could conceive of asking each individual how much he would be willing to pay to avoid the noise. While such a complete survey is often not feasible, that is not even the main problem. The main problem is getting individuals to reveal their true valuations. Each person who opposes the construction of the airport is motivated to exaggerate the noise costs, whereas each person who favors it is motivated to understate it.

In CBA, the analyst can deal with externalities in a number of ways, none of which is completely satisfactory:

(a)   Conduct a survey of WTP among the affected individuals and hope that true preferences are revealed, or that the exaggerations cancel out the understatements.

(b)   As an estimate of WTP, compute the costs of avoiding the externality, such as the costs of sound insulation for homes and autos or ear plugs for being outdoors. This is neither an upper bound nor a lower bound on the true cost. For example, avoidance costs may be $3000, but one person may value silence at $10,000 while another values it at $100. The fact that it would cost the airport administration only $3000 to give the first individual the silence he values at $10,000 does not diminish the fact that the lack of silence is a *cost of $10,000* to that person. Thus, the avoidance cost has no special significance to a CBA beyond its intuitive appeal as a reasonable number to look at, and perhaps as an indicator of the order of magnitude of the true cost.

(c)   Compute the critical value of the externality. All the social benefits and all *other* social costs can be computed to yield a net social value of the project before the inclusion of the value of the externality. Thus, if the value is already negative, or lower than some alternative project, the project is definitely not worth undertaking, and an exact computation of the loss resulting from the externality need not be attempted. If the value turns out to be positive, then a critical value can be computed for the externality, and the judgment can be left to the decision maker as to whether the actual social cost of the externality exceeds the critical value. For example, in the airport noise problem, suppose that the net social value of the airport, exclusive of noise considerations, is 10 million dollars. The decision maker then must judge whether that figure outweighs or is outweighed by, the social cost of the noise.

(d) As a last resort, only a qualitative description of the impact of the externality can be presented to the decision maker. This effectively shifts the burden of analysis from the analyst to the decision maker. It is not recommended except when all quantitative methods fail.

5.4.2 Public Goods

Public goods are goods which are consumed jointly by individuals. Formally, a public good has the following characteristics:

(a) Consumption of such a good is nonrival, that is, one person's consumption does not diminish the amount available to any other person.

(b) It is not feasible (and sometimes not even possible) to exclude any individual from consuming the good, once the good is provided.

Examples of public goods include national defense, mosquito control activities, light houses, bridges, and parks.[4] Many other exhibit "publicness" to lesser, but still significant, degrees. These goods include police and fire services, and fireworks displays on the 4th of July.

Since it is not feasible—at a reasonable cost—to exclude any person from consuming a public good, it follows that no firm is likely to find it profitable to supply public goods to the market since the firm would have to rely on *voluntary* contributions for its revenues. Payments for private (nonpublic) goods are not voluntary insofar as one *must* pay to receive the good. Here, owing to nonexcludability, one receives the good whether or not one pays. Therefore, it is indeed possible to simultaneously observe a demand for some good and an absence of firms willing to supply the good. In such situations, governments undertake to provide the goods, and finance this provision through taxes. In general, there is no precise relation between the taxes one pays and the public goods one consumes. One tax payment to a government unit will go toward the payment for a variety of government services. For example, a local property tax may finance local education, police and fire services, street lighting, and road maintenance. The point of all this is that there is no meaningful per unit "price" to the individual for the consumption of public goods. This lack of price means a lack of an objective yardstick of value for public goods. Therefore, when a public project affects the quantity of some public good, the cost–benefit analyst is faced with the difficult problem of determining the value of that good without any guidance from objective measures of value, such as market prices.

The modern economic theory of public goods was formulated by Paul Samuelson (1954, 1955) in a series of articles in the mid-1950s. The theory is interesting because it simultaneously provides a specific formula for determining the value of a public good to an individual and then explains why this formula can never be actually applied. (This, by the way, is no shortcoming of the theory. It results from an appreciation of human avarice.) It

---

[4] Bridges and parks are public goods as long as crowding of the facilities does not occur.

is important that the analyst, charged with valuing public goods, be familiar with this theory, if only so he knows what his approximations should be approximations to.

For expositional ease, we develop the theory in the context of an economy with one public good and three consumers. Once the general principles are discovered, extension to more realistic cases is straightforward. First, we assume that we can meaningfully express the units of measurement for the public good, for example, the number of acres in a park, soldiers in an army, or mosquitos killed. In Figure 5.12 let S represent the supply curve of the economy for the public good, and assume that the prices correspond to shadow prices. Here D^α, D^β, and D^δ are the demands for the public good by the three consumers; D is the market demand curve derived by adding the individual demands *vertically*. This is in contrast to the horizontal addition of demand curves for private goods. The optimal amount of the public good the government should provide is Q^*, determined by the intersection of S and D. To see this, consider the alternatives. If some amount less than Q^* were provided, say $\bar{Q}$, the total WTP for one extra unit would be $\bar{P}$, whereas the cost to society (the three consumers) of providing that extra unit would be P^0. Since $\bar{P}$

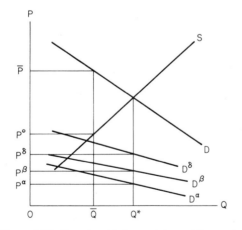

Figure 5.12   Supply and demand for public goods.

exceeds P^0, total social welfare is increased by providing that marginal unit. This argument applies to any value of Q less than Q^*. That is, whenever the amount provided is less than Q^*, society's welfare can be increased by increasing Q. A similar argument shows that if more than Q^* were provided, society could increase its welfare by decreasing that amount. Therefore, Q^* is the optimal amount of the public good since any deviation from Q^* causes a drop in welfare.

How should Q^* be financed? A reasonable criterion is that each individual should pay in proportion to the benefits he receives, which are expressed by his WTP. Thus, from the individual demand curves, we see that when Q^* units are provided, consumers α, β, and δ are willing to pay

$$P^\alpha + P^\beta + P^\delta = P.$$

The result is that the optimal amount of the public good can be determined, and it can be financed by assessing individuals on the basis of the WTP reflected in their demand curves.

With regard to CBA, it would appear that we have a clear-cut method for determining the value of a public good to an individual—simply refer to the individual's demand curve for a measure of WTP.

But this is the catch! In general, there is no way to get an individual to reveal his true WTP for a public good. For private goods, true WTP is revealed by the consumer's purchases of various quantities at various prices, that is, through the market. But public goods are not traded in a market (owing to their nonexcludability property, discussed above), and so WTP is not revealed by behavior. Why not simply approach consumers and put the matter before them: "The government is considering providing a 50-acre park in this area, how much would you be willing to pay to get such a park?" The park, incidentally, will be financed by general tax revenues.

How can we expect the consumers to respond? If they favor the idea, they would try to increase the chance of its being adopted. Since they know that they are not going to be assessed the amount they state, they probably will respond with an exaggerated figure. If they are against the idea, even though the park would yield some benefits, they probably will understate their WTP.

At this point, the reader might object that we should have told the consumers that they will be assessed in proportion to the amount they claim. That should force them to be more truthful, particularly if they favor the project. Let us analyze how a consumer might respond in that situation, assuming that the consumer favors the project. First, the consumer definitely would not exaggerate the value that he would get from the park. If he did, and the park were provided, he would suffer a net loss. The remaining alternatives are to tell the truth or to understate the true WTP. Recognizing these alternatives, the individual will assume that everyone else will also consider them when responding. It is convenient to use the "game" matrix shown as Table 5.3 to represent the individuals' decision problem. The individual has two strategies—tell the truth or understate. He assumes that "everyone else" has the same options. As the matrix indicates, there are four possible outcomes, or "payoffs" to the individual. Suppose that the value to the individual is 100 if he and everyone tell the true WTP.[5] On the other hand, suppose that he understates WTP, and everyone else tells the truth. Then he still gets a park, and in addition saves some money. This outcome is clearly superior to the former—say, its valued at 140. If the consumer tells the truth, and everyone else understates WTP, the con-

TABLE 5.3
Illustration of an Individual's Decision Matrix in Public Goods Analysis

		Everyone else's strategies	
		Truth	Understate
Individual's	Truth	100	80
strategies	Understate	140	100

[5] The values in the matrix are expected values. Since total WTP may exceed actual cost, they may not be asked to contribute their entire stated WTP. Furthermore, the payoffs assume that the park is built. If it is not built, there is neither loss nor gain.

sumer's assessment will be closer to his stated WTP. Certainly, the value of this outcome must be less than that obtained when everyone, including the consumer, tells the truth. Suppose it is worth 80. Finally, suppose everyone, including the consumer, understates the value. Then the proportional assessment will tend to be the same as that obtained when everyone tells the truth. Value it also at 100.

Let us now determine the rational strategy for the individual. Clearly it is to understate WTP for, no matter what everyone else does, understating always yields the highest payoff. If everyone perceives the situation as does this individual, everyone is motivated to understate his or her true WTP. Thus, a straightforward inquiry addressed to individuals does not hold much promise in eliciting true responses concerning the value of public goods for CBA.[6]

5.5 SUMMARY

To summarize, the theory of public goods outlined above suggests that assessing individuals on the basis of their WTP can lead to an optimal provision of public goods. Unfortunately, there is no foolproof method to get individuals to reveal their WTP. Their retorts, it is reasonably feared, may easily be biased by strategic considerations.

What is the cost–benefit analyst to do? Once again, there is no completely satisfactory approach. However, approaches usually followed include:

(a) Surveys, where the questions are asked in a manner disguising their purpose. The problem still remains that

---

[6] It should be obvious that the specific numbers used in the game matrix are irrelevant, as long as they bear the proper directional inequality relation to one another. Behavior of the sort predicted by this game is called the "free-rider" problem.

responses to survey questions may not be based on careful consideration of one's own values.

(b) Analogy to private goods. Where the public good is related to some marketed good, the price of the latter may be a guide to the value of the former.

(c) Experiments. Individuals might be asked to participate in "realistic" games designed to reveal their true preferences. Such information is costly, and usually of questionable reliability.

(d) Public referenda which provide a number of output–cost levels to vote on, and where the means of financing the project can reasonably be claimed to be currently unknown. Since no one knows how the costs will be shared, it is hoped the votes do not reflect strategic behavior. While this method might be useful for determining the most preferred level of output, it does not ascertain whether the net social value, even at that level, is positive.

Note: In certain types of economic studies, it is frequently assumed that the cost of providing a good is equal to the value of consuming the good. Such an assumption must *never* be made in CBA, for it clearly sidesteps the whole problem of determining whether benefits exceed costs.

6
THE DISCOUNT RATE

. . . Things without all remedy
Should be without regard: what's done is done.

Shakespeare, *Macbeth, Act iii, scene 2, 1.11*

6.1 INTRODUCTION

Invariably, a project subjected to a CBA will have its costs
and benefits spread over a number of years. In order to compare
one project with another, or to determine the economic viability
of a particular project, one must reduce the time stream of costs
and benefits to a single number. Most often, this aggregation
over time is accomplished by computing the net present value
(NPV) of a project. The reader will recall that NPV and related
terms were discussed in Chapter 2. The NPV approach discounts
future net benefits to their present value. Clearly, the rate of
discount is a crucial parameter in the NPV calculation.[1] In the
evaluation of a single project, the discount rate will affect
whether the NPV is greater or less than zero. In a comparison of

[1] Indeed, every other reasonable decision measure (such as the benefit–cost
ratio or the internal rate of return) also depends critically on the chosen discount
rate.

projects, the discount rate will affect their NPV ranking. This last statement may not be obvious, for it may be thought that, while the chosen discount rate affects the magnitude of NPV, it does not affect the ranking of projects. This fallacious notion is easily dispelled by an example. Projects A and B each last three years. Their annual net benefits (that is, each entry is total annual benefits less total annual cost) are:

		Net benefits		
	Initial cost	Year 1	Year 2	Year 3
Project A	−100	220.0	12.1	13.3
Project B	−100	0	0	266.0

Project A has a large initial return that tapers off over time. Project B has net benefits occurring only in the terminal year. Now let us calculate NPV for each project at discount rates of 1 and 10%. The results are:

	NPV at 1%	NPV at 10%
Project A	143	120
Project B	158	100

Note that B is superior to A at a discount rate of 1%, but A is superior to B at a discount rate of 10%. Thus, the discount rate obviously can affect the ranking of projects. High discount rates penalize projects with benefits occurring farther in the future.

One of the truly interesting controversies that has developed in CBA revolves around the choice of the proper discount rate to use in the present value calculations of CBA. As seen above, the value chosen can easily tilt the scales away from one project and toward another. The controversy is not over numerical values per se, although that is surely part of the issue; rather, it concerns the very concept of what the discount rate ought to measure. The correct discount rate, which we shall term the *social discount rate*, is that rate which, when applied to future costs and benefits, yields their actual present social values. In other words, the proper rate is the rate at which society as a whole is willing to trade off present for future costs and benefits. The problems one encounters are twofold. First, how does one translate this definition into an operational context? That is, which of the myriad conceptual rates, if any, accurately measures this proper rate? Second, once the conceptual rate is agreed on, which of the many values it achieves is the correct value? Since the debate still rages over the first question, not much has been established about the second. Thus, our discussion in this chapter deals almost exclusively with identifying and investigating various conceptual approaches to isolation of the true social discount rate. The discussion proceeds in two parts: an overview of the various conceptual rates, followed by an investigation of the merits of various arguments espousing one or another, or some combination, of the conceptual rates.

6.2 DISCOUNT RATE CONCEPTS

The rate concepts we list and briefly discuss include market interest rates, the marginal productivity of investment, the corporate discount rate, the government borrowing rate, the Pigouvian rate, and the social opportunity cost of capital.

6.2.1 Market Interest Rates

These rates are distinguished by their multiplicity. They are associated chiefly with corporate and government bonds and with the debt instruments of financial institutions such as commercial banks and savings and loan associations. Corporate and government bonds are, of course, vehicles for borrowing funds. When corporations or municipalities wish to undertake a large investment, they often choose to borrow some or all the necessary money. They do this by selling bonds. While there are many minor variations among bonds regarding the rights of, and

conditions placed on, the borrower and lender, essentially a
bond is the promise of the borrower to pay Y dollars to the lender
T years from now in exchange for the lender giving the borrower
X dollars now. Of course, Y is always greater than X. Given X, Y,
and T, it is possible to compute the interest rate that the
borrower is effectively paying or, equally, the interest rate that
the lender is effectively earning. Denoting the interest rate as i, it
is that i which solves

$$X = \frac{Y}{(1 + i)^T}.$$

For example, if $X = \$1000$, $Y = \$2000$, and $T = 10$, then $i = 7.18\%$. Alternatively, when a financial institution lends money,
the interest rate ordinarily is explicitly stated.

Many different rates are observed simultaneously in the
market place due to differences in the *risk* that the lender is
taking. Clearly, the greater the risk (that the borrower will default
on his payment), the greater the interest that the lender will
demand in order to persuade him (the lender) to make the loan.

6.2.2 Marginal Productivity of Investment

This *is* the *real* rate of return that the economy's marginal
investment projects yield. By "real" is meant the market value of
the outputs and net of all the inputs of the project, both
appropriately discounted for time. For example, if the *least
profitable* (hence, marginal) investment projects undertaken in
the economy give an annual net return of $6 for a $100 initial
investment, then the marginal productivity of investment is 6%.
This means that, if extra investment funds were made available,
and if they were invested in the private sector, a 6% return
would be realized by the economy. Likewise, if investment funds
were withdrawn from the private sector, a return of 6% would be
foregone by the economy.

6.2.3 The Corporate Discount Rate

This is the rate used by a corporation to evaluate potential investment projects. It includes both a risk premium and a "markup" for corporate taxes. Since a corporation faces a federal tax rate of approximately 50%, its before-tax earnings must be double its desired after-tax earnings. Of course, in order for a corporation to attract investors, its aftertax earnings must be competitive with alternative investments open to potential stockholders in the corporation. Thus, if riskless government bonds have a return of 6%, and allowing a 3% risk premium, a corporation must offer stockholders a return on the order of 9% as an inducement for investing their capital. Thus, a gross return of around 18% is required.

The implication of this line of reasoning for government investment is ominous. The opportunity cost of foregone corporate investment projects is, perhaps, 15–20%. Should not government projects be evaluated at similar rates to avoid resource misallocation? This question is investigated later in this chapter.

6.2.4 The Government Borrowing Rate

This is the rate at which the government borrows money from the private sector; thus, it is the "cost" of government borrowing. The reasonableness of this rate for use in CBA derives from the inescapable conclusion that, since some individuals are willing to lend money to the government at, say 6%, they must feel better off receiving their money back plus 6% at some time in the future than they do in using (consuming) their money now. Therefore, if a government project has a return of 6% or more, consumers are better off if the project is undertaken.

6.2.5 The Own Personal Discount Rate

The rate at which an individual is willing to trade off his own present consumption for his own future consumption may

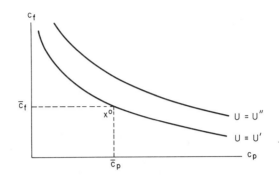

Figure 6.1   Indifference curves of a two-period intertemporal utility function.

be termed their *own personal discount rate*.[2] For example, a rate of 10% would mean that the individual would give up $1.00 in consumption in this time period if he were compensated with a minimum of $1.10 in consumption in the next period. He would accept more than $1.10, of course, but would not accept less. A graphic interpretation is quite straightforward. Consider a consumer who must distribute his consumption possibilities between two periods, the present and the future. Denote the amount consumed in each period by c_p and c_f, respectively; $U(c_p, c_f)$ is his utility function, expressing his preferences over present and future consumption. It is usually (and reasonably) assumed that the indifference curves generated by $U(c_p, c_f)$ are convex to the origin, as shown in Figure 6.1. The term U'' represents a higher level of utility than U'. Suppose that the consumer finds himself at X^0, presently consuming $\bar{c}_p$ and anticipating $\bar{c}_f$ in the future period. Suppose further that, for some reason, he is asked to consume $1 less in the present period in exchange for α in the future. What is the minimum α acceptable to the consumer? Since the consumer will voluntarily accept no offer that makes him worse off, he will insist on retaining a utility level of at least

---

[2] Strictly speaking, we should call it the "own personal marginal discount rate." The rate depends on the current intertemporal distribution of consumption, and our interest is in marginal changes from that base.

U'. Thus, our interest is in

$$\frac{\Delta c_f}{\Delta c_p} \quad \text{along} \quad U', \quad\quad\quad (6.1)$$

that is, the change in c_f necessary to stay on U' when there is a change in c_p. Of course, Equation (6.1) is nothing more than the slope of U' at X. Equally, Equation (6.1) is an expression of the own personal discount rate.[3] This shows that, graphically, the own personal discount rate is the slope of the consumer's intertemporal indifference curve evaluated at the current consumption distribution.

6.2.6 The Own Social Discount Rate

The *own social discount rate* stands in interesting contrast to the own private discount rate. While the latter reflects one's own preferences for one's *own* behavior, the former reflects one's own preferences for *social* behavior. It is not at all unlikely that these two rates will differ for any individual, as is discussed later in this chapter.

The own social discount rate is an *individual's* judgment as to the correct growth path for real per capita consumption in the economy. In Figure 6.2 are illustrated several types of feasible growth profiles. The profile AH calls for a high rate of growth in consumption. However, since all consumption is at the expense of investment,[4] capital stocks are diminished, and capacity to produce falls. A high initial growth in AH is paid for by low consumption in later periods. An individual who favors paths like AH has a high own social discount rate, for a high rate weights the immediate future heavily and the distant future

---

[3] For example, $\Delta c_f = \$1.10$ when $\Delta c_p = \$1.00$ indicates the own personal discount rate is 10%. Thus, the slope of U' at X is -1.10.

[4] Recall the basic GNP account equation: $Y \equiv C + I + G$, where Y, C, I, and G are GNP, consumption, investment, and government spending, respectively. $C + G$ may be viewed as private plus public consumption. Thus, for given Y, more $C + G$ means less I.

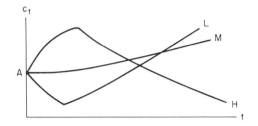

Figure 6.2   Feasible per-capita consumption growth paths.

lightly. In contrast to *AH* is *AL*. To achieve this stream, consumption must be sacrificed in the immediate future. The payoff is
higher consumption opportunities in the more distant future. If
an individual prefers *AL*, his own social discount rate is low, for
he prefers to weigh the future heavily. The profile *AM* provides
for slow but steady growth.

Why might the own social discount rate differ from the own
personal discount rate? Consider an example. Suppose that an
individual currently has a high income and, through existing
contractual agreements, knows that he will maintain a high
income for the next ten years. That individual's income after
these ten years is uncertain, but the general state of the economy
after ten years will certainly be an important determinant. If the
economy is doing well at that time, then the individual expects
that he will do well; if not, not. On the other hand, the state of
the economy during these next ten years is not of importance, for
the individual's income is guaranteed. This individual might
well choose path *AL* of Figure 6.2, that is, a low own social
discount rate, even though his own personal discount rate may
be high. The own social discount rate depends heavily on one's
anticipated income stream and its dependence on the general
state of the economy. Again, there is no reason to expect an own
personal discount rate to coincide with an own social discount
rate.[5]

---

[5] Note that the own social discount rate is a surrogate measure of the *timing*
of projects. In the example, the individual's goal was to match an economic boom
with the expiration of his guaranteed income. Expressing a desire for a low social
discount rate is one, albeit imperfect, way to attempt to achieve his goal.

6.2.7 The Pigouvian Discount Rate

A. C. Pigou, a noted British welfare economist, observed that individuals have faulty "telescopic" vision concerning the future, and are inclined not to make sufficient provision for it. Individuals weigh themselves too heavily and future generations too lightly. Because future generations are unrepresented now, their interests are not well regarded. Pigou (1946) suggested that it is the government's task to correct this bias favoring present generations. Government must view itself as the trustee of future. Thus, in evaluating public investment projects, government should impose a lower discount rate than shortsighted individuals would now (selfishly) deem best.

6.3 THE SOCIAL DISCOUNT RATE

The social discount rate is the term for *the* proper discount rate to employ in cost-benefit analyses. Candidate rates for designation as the social discount rate include those discussed above. In this section we present some arguments that various authors have developed espousing one rate or another.

6.3.1 The Argument for a Low Social Discount Rate[6]

Consonant with Pigou's (1946) observation about the shortsightedness of individuals, some economists have argued that a low social discount rate should be adopted. This would enable projects with benefits occurring farther in the future to prove more acceptable. For example, suppose that a project's only cost is an initial one of $1000, and suppose that the only benefit, $3000, occurs 20 years in the future. At a discount rate of .10, the net present value of the project is −$544; however, at a rate of .05 the net present value is $141. Clearly, a low social discount rate

[6] The material in this section is based on Marglin (1963a).

extols the virtues of projects with payoffs occurring in the more distant future.

The argument for a low (where "low" means lower than market rates) social discount rate rests on the difference between an individual's preferences in his capacity as an individual, and his preferences as a member of a society capable of collective action.

A simple model will illustrate the relevant points best. First, let us define some notation:

c is the level of present consumption for an individual,

c_f the level of consumption enjoyed by an individual in the "future,"

c_p the level of consumption for the present generation,

U the utility index for the individual,

k the marginal rate of transformation between the present and future (an investment of I_0 now returns kI_0 in the future), and

α, β the positive constants.

We begin by assuming that the (representative) individual receives satisfaction from his own present consumption, the rest of society's present consumption, and the anticipated consumption by the future. Thus

$$U = U(c, c_p - c, c_f). \tag{6.2}$$

The total differential of Equation (6.2)

$$dU = \frac{\partial U}{\partial c}dc = \frac{\partial U}{\partial(c_p - c)}d(c_p - c) + \frac{\partial U}{\partial c_f}dc_f. \tag{6.3}$$

For simplicity, assume that the partial derivatives are constants over the relevant range, and further assume the utility index is scaled so $\partial U/\partial c = 1$.[7] Equation (6.3) may be rewritten as

$$dU = dc + \alpha\, d(c_p - c) + \beta\, dc_f. \tag{6.4}$$

[7] Modern economic theory considers the utility function to be ordinal, rather than cardinal, in nature. Thus, any monotonic transformation of a utility function is itself a valid representation of the underlying preferences the utility function represents. All the important results of economic theory that depend on utility functions may be derived from ordinal utility relations.

Now suppose that this individual is considering investing $1 for the benefit of future generations. He will do this only if dU resulting from this action is greater than or equal to zero. The action involves both costs and benefits to himself. The cost is a decrease in his own present consumption of $1, so $dc = -1$. The benefit is the increase in future consumption by k, so $dc_f = k$. Overall,

$$dU = -1 + \beta k \qquad (6.5)$$

The investment will be undertaken if $dU \geq 0$, or $\beta k \geq 1$. Consider some "likely" values for β and k. For most individuals, we might say that a β of .03–.05 would be a generous guess. In fact, one might argue for "typical" β's of less than .01. How about k? Perhaps values of 2 or 3, even 4 or 5, might be advanced. In almost any case, however, it is extremely unlikely that the product of β and k will equal or exceed unity. We conclude that, for the most part, individuals faced with a choice of investing for the benefit of the future or not investing will find their interests best served by not investing. This conclusion depends on the premise that the individual is choosing as an individual.

Now consider the possibility of collective action. By *collective action* is meant that all individuals bind themselves to pursue the same course. Thus, either no one invests for the benefit of the future, or all do. Suppose that the issue will be put to a vote. An individual will vote yes (let us all invest for future) or no (let us all not invest), depending, again, on his own dU. He still bases his determination on his own best interests, but now the realm of choice is changed. By agreeing to subjugate his own will to the will of (let us say) the majority, he is guaranteed that all will act in unison, if not in harmony. Let there be N members of society. The option that the individual now considers is that each must give up $1 in present consumption and invest it for the benefit of the future. Thus,

$$dc = -1,$$
$$dc_p = -N,$$
$$dc_f = kN.$$

Then

$$dU = -1 - \alpha(N - 1) + \beta kN. \tag{6.6}$$

The term dU equals or exceeds zero if

$$N(\beta k - \alpha) \geq 1 - \alpha. \tag{6.7}$$

Assuming that α has magnitude similar to β, the right-hand side of Equation (6.7) is close to 1. For N on the order of hundreds, thousands, or even millions, the left-hand side is *very likely* to be greater than or equal to the other.[8] We can conclude that in a collective choice situation, a representative individual will be very likely to favor investing for the future.

Thus far, we have established that an individual's decision to invest for the future will probably differ, depending on whether the choice situation is individualistic or collective. However, we have not determined which of the choice situations is to be preferred. Will the individual fare better or worse when the choice is collective? Fortunately, a simple comparison of Equation (6.5) with Equation (6.7) provides the answer. The individual will prefer the decision to be made collectively as long as

$$-1 - \alpha(N - 1) + \beta kN > -1 + \beta k \tag{6.8}$$

or, equally,

$$\beta k - \alpha > 0. \tag{6.9}$$

Interestingly, the preference for the collective mode of choice does not depend on N, the number of persons bound by the collective choice. As we argued above, Equation (6.9) is likely to hold. Therefore, individuals are better off if decisions involving investments for the future are made collectively, rather than individually. Looked at another way, individuals have more concern for the future than their behavior as individuals suggests. As individuals, they would choose not to invest for the

[8] It would seem, for very large N, a virtually sufficient condition for $dU > 0$ is $\beta k - \alpha > 0$. For β and α of similar magnitudes this is quite likely. Only if the individual feels very much more altruistic toward his contemporaries than toward the future will $\beta k - \alpha > 0$ fail to hold.

future. However, if collective action could be arranged, individuals *would invest and feel better off* having done so.

We have said nothing thus far about discount rates. What implication does the foregoing development hold for the social discount rate? Market interest rates arise through the interaction of the forces of the supply and demand of loanable funds. These rates indicate each individual's rate of trading off present for future income. Equally, it is the discount rate that individuals apply to future income. But market interest rates reflect the trade-offs individuals make as individuals. If the market interest rate reflects the discount rate that individuals, acting individually, apply to the future, then by all the preceding arguments, individuals collectively value the future more than that market rate suggests. Hence, the proper rate to use in CBA—the social discount rate—must be lower than the market rate. A lower market rate gives greater weight to the future than does a higher rate.

6.3.2 The Argument for a Low Social Discount Rate (Continued)

For readers familiar with elementary game theory, the foregoing conclusion can be developed in the context of the theory of games. Consider the following decision (or game) matrix. We assume the individual does get satisfaction from knowing that future society will "inherit" goods the present society has provided through investment, that is, through devoting current resources to projects that will pay benefits in the future, even though those in the present are deprived of some consumption opportunities. The individual may feel this way for any number of reasons, for example:

(1) the individual may be part of the future society,
(2) the individual's children and other relatives may be part of that society, or
(3) the individual may have a general feeling of altruism toward mankind.

For simplicity, assume that the representative individual has two choices: invest for the future (I), or do not invest for the future (DI). Likewise, he perceives that society as a whole has those same choices. Suppose his "payoff" is 100 when both he and the rest of society invest for the future. If the rest of society invests and he does not, he is even better off; he has the satisfaction of knowing that the future is being prepared for, without personally foregoing any present consumption. Say this value is 150. The converse situation—the individual invests and society does not, is the worst possible one. Not only do future members of society get nothing (since that lone contribution has a negligible impact in the future), but the individual has foregone present consumption. Let us value this outcome at −50. If society chooses DI and the individual does also, at least he has not given up present consumption and he is clearly better off than −50. However, since he loses the satisfaction of knowing the future is being provided for, he gets less than 100 from this outcome. Say the (DI, DI) payoff is 25. These choices and their values to the individual are summarized in the following payoff matrix:

Representative individual's choices	Society's choices	
	Invest	Do not invest
Invest	100	−50
Do not invest	150	25

Now let us analyze the investment decision in two contrasting contexts: a private investment decision and a public investment decision. Suppose, for concreteness, that both investments involve the purchase of land that is currently unusable but will be a beautiful natural area 25 years in the future, for example, swamp land where drainage is expected with certainty. The individual would like to dedicate the small tract he purchases as a wildlife refuge. He realizes, however, that as an individual he has no control over what society will do with the adjoining land 25 years hence. Thus, his "wildlife refuge" of several acres may turn out to be surrounded by a land fill (that is, the individual invests for the future and society does not). On the other hand, if everyone else buys the land to keep it natural, and he does not, his marginal acres will not make much difference. The above decision matrix, as the reader will note, has straightforward applications. The individual's rational choice must be DI, since the payoff is higher for DI, no matter what the rest of society does. That is, the individual will decide not to purchase the land for dedication as a natural area. Such private decisions about provision for the future seem to imply that individuals have a "high" discount rate for future goods. That is what private investment decisions would seem to imply, and this would be reflected in the data. For instance, the data would show that at current market interest rates, individuals do not feel that this investment is worthwhile.

However, now suppose that the individual can affect society's choice. That is, suppose the matter of what to do with all the land is to be decided by a public vote. If the majority decides to purchase the land for a natural state, the purchase will be financed by taxes. Now each individual will consider the decision from society's viewpoint. Only the (I, I) and (DI, DI) choices are now feasible. The rational social choice is clearly I—to invest. That is, by a public decision to invest, each individual in effect forces the rest of society to choose I, in return for which he, himself is forced to choose I. Thus, each person can be assured of a payoff of 100. The rational choice of society to invest in the land means that its discount rate, the *social* discount rate, must be lower than the discount rate reflected by private decisions. The example shows that in the case of this type of investment for the future, *everyone is made better off by having the decision made with reference to the social discount rate rather than the individual discount rate. The social discount rate is lower than the individual rate, and it is reflected only in public decisions.* At the risk of being repetitive, we must stress that this social rate cannot be derived from the data on individual investment decisions. Operationally, what all this argument means is that market interest rates, which reflect individual investment decisions, are no guide to the correct discount rate for CBA, except as an upper bound.[9]

[9] The normative significance of market interest rates is obscured further by the realization that market rates are manipulated by federal policies (for example, stabilization, employment, foreign exchange) for reasons far removed from long-term public investment decisions.

6.3.3 The Argument for a High Social Discount Rate[10]

The true opportunity costs of a government project must be considered in the CBA of that project. By opportunity cost is meant what members of society give up, now and in the future, in order to accomplish the project. This uncontestable premise is the basis for the arguments espousing a high social discount rate. While these arguments are remarkably straightforward, they are best developed in the context of a simple model. Assume that all goods in the economy are supplied either by government or by corporations. With public goods being provided by the government, all private goods are thus produced and sold by firms organized as corporations. Assume that corporate profits are taxed at a uniform rate of 50%, and that corporations are financed entirely by equity. Finally, assume that there exists a single constant rate r at which the government borrows money.

Now suppose that consideration is being given to the undertaking of a public investment project. What discount rate should be applied to net present value (NPV) calculation? The discount rate should be such that NPV > 0 if and only if the benefits outweigh the true opportunity costs of the investment. That is, the discount rate should reflect the opportunity costs of using the resources in the public project. The opportunity costs, of course, are the returns that could be earned by those resources in the private sector. Simply put, resources should be steered into their most gainful use. If the public sector investment project is not the best use of the resources, then it should not show a nonnegative NPV.

Following this opportunity cost argument, it appears that the bench mark against which to measure the returns of the public project is the returns that can be achieved in the private sector. Using the model described above, let us attempt to infer the marginal rate of return earned by private sector investments. First, we note that individuals in our simple economy have two investment alternatives: the purchase of government bonds or

[10] The material in this section draws on Baumol (1968).

the purchase of corporate stocks. The former are completely free of risk, yielding a certain rate of return r. The latter, however, are not risk free. In order to attract stockholders' equity, a rate in excess of r must be offered by the corporation. That is, because stockholders face the possibilities of losses in their stock purchases, they demand a *risk premium* to induce them to purchase corporate equity. Thus, a rate of return must be paid to investors equal to $r + \bar{r}$, where $\bar{r}$ is the risk premium. For example, if $r = 6\%$, and if $\bar{r} = 2\%$, then stockholders demand and receive a net rate of return of 8% on stocks.

Now what can be said about marginal corporate investment projects? Since the corporation must pay 50% of its net earnings in taxes, the marginal investment project must have a before-tax return of $2(r + \bar{r})$. Only with this return is an investment profitable. For example, where $r = 6\%$, and $\bar{r} = 2\%$, the marginal corporate investment project must have a before-tax return of 16%. Of that, half (8%) is paid in taxes, and half (8%) is the stockholders' return. The stockholders' return may be distributed as dividends or retained by the corporation. In the latter case, the value of the stockholder's equity would increase by 8%. It is clear that the corporate money would be lost if any project were pursued yielding less than 16% *and* if there was failure to pursue any investment project yielding more than 16%. Again, the marginal corporate investment project has a rate of return of $2(r + \bar{r})$. This is the bench mark against which public investment projects must be measured. That is, the *opportunity cost* of public investment is $2(r + \bar{r})$, which is the rate that should be used in NPV calculations for public projects.

Two objections may be raised to this line of reasoning:

(a) Not all public investment is, dollar for dollar, in lieu of private investment. Indeed, it is reasonable to expect that, had tax monies not been raised to fund the public project, more private consumption and private investment would have occurred. Perhaps the public investment project largely replaces private consumption. Does not this possibility void the foregoing opportunity cost argument?

(b) The existence of risk in corporate investment means that some of the projects will not achieve their expected $2(r + \bar{r})$ rate of return. In fact, some will have a return of substantially less. Should not the opportunity cost rate of $2(r + \bar{r})$ be reduced because of the presence of risk?

Both of these objections can be dismissed. With regard to the first, the opportunity cost rate of $2(r + \bar{r})$ does not depend on private investment being supplanted. Indeed, suppose that only private consumption is supplanted by the public investment project. In this case, consumers have voluntarily foregone $(r + \bar{r})$ paid by corporations in order to enjoy present consumption. Moreover, the $(r + \bar{r})$ the consumer would have reaped from the purchase of stocks would be equaled by a $(r + \bar{r})$ tax collection by the government [since the total return is $2(r + \bar{r})$] and, presumably, the provision of $(r + \bar{r})$ worth of public goods by the government. Again, the value of the foregone consumption is on the order of $2(r + \bar{r})$. It does not matter whether private consumption or investment is supplanted. There is still an opportunity cost of $2(r + \bar{r})$.

In the second objection it is asked whether the presence of risk should penalize the opportunity cost rate rather than enhance it. The key to this issue is in the recognition that both individual public and private projects are risky. The actual value of any given proposed project, public or private, may deviate from what was expected. However, over a large number of projects, if we can assume similar variances in their expected returns, the deviations from the expectations tend to wash out and, on average, society receives the expected values of the projects. A risk factor enters into the calculation of corporate returns because the individual corporation is typically not so large that it can pursue a sufficient number of projects so that it is (virtually) assured their expected value. While the returns to any given corporation are uncertain (risky), the returns to the entire corporate sector are virtually certain, and equal the expected returns. Likewise, because of the large public sector, the overall returns to public projects equal their expected values. Since it is the overall returns to society in which we are interested, there is no more risk in corporate projects than in government projects. There is no reason to penalize one or the other because of risk. In sum, while the presence of risk in the calculus of individual corporations causes them to fail to pursue projects with expected returns less than $2(r + \bar{r})$, the return on the large number of projects pursued by the corporate sector is nonetheless a (virtually) certain $2(r - \bar{r})$. Given this degree of certainty, there is no cause to penalize the rate of return because of risk. (Indeed, any risk that remains in the corporate sector must also be present in the public sector. If one is penalized, both must be.) The opportunity cost of public investment remains at $2(r + \bar{r})$.

That this line of reasoning supports "high" social discount rates is clear. While the previous section concluded that the social discount rate should be less than the market rate, this section concludes that it should be at least twice that rate. Operationally, this amounts to a very significant difference because cost–benefit results are extremely responsive to the discount rate employed.

6.3.4 A Composite Approach to the Social Discount Rate: The Social Opportunity Cost of Capital[11]

In principle, it is possible to simultaneously employ the sense of both preceding arguments in a single composite approach to discounting. The first argument demands that the future be given more weight than market rates allow, and the second argument demands that the true opportunity cost of government investment projects be considered. The key to making the overtly conflicting viewpoints compatible is the representation of opportunity costs in the dollar costs of the project rather than in the discount rate. Thus, the discount rate may be set "low," but the costs of the project, measured as the "social opportunity cost of capital" (SOCC), are "large."

The SOCC refers to the welfare loss borne by society when

---

[11] The material in this section draws on Marglin (1963b).

resources are transferred from the private to the public sector. Analytically, the approach may be classified as a form of "multiplier analysis" since the object of the analysis is to determine the SOCC used in a project by the relation

$$SOCC = M \times R,$$

where R is the capital cost of the project and M is a multiplier greater than 1.

This approach rests on the hypotheses that funds transferred from the private sector to finance a project represent a greater real cost to society than simply counting dollar costs would imply. The reasoning is that the transfer of funds reduces both consumption and investment in the initial period. The reduced investment causes a lower-than-otherwise level of national income in succeeding years, and consequently a lower level of consumption in those years. The quite legitimate argument is made that this lower-than-otherwise consumption is the real (welfare) social cost of the project.

In more formal terms, then, let us consider the time stream of consumption which society would enjoy in the absence of the project. Denote this consumption stream by

$$C_0, C_1, C_2, \ldots, C_t, \ldots, C_T.$$

This consumption stream is associated with a corresponding stream of savings which are invested to maintain the consumption stream in future periods. By drawing resources from the private sector, a public project reduces private investment. This private investment would have had a positive effect over the years. That is, investment today would produce a continuous stream of returns (income) in the future. In each of these years, investment is further increased because of the higher income level. Thus, each year gives rise to its own stream of extra consumption in the future. For example, in the fifth year, consumption includes that generated by investments in the first, second, third, and fourth years. Thus, the argument states that all these consumption streams are foregone by the transfer of funds to the government. Denote the resultant time stream of consumption by

$$C_0', C_1', C_2', \ldots, C_t', \ldots, C_T'.$$

This time stream is *net* of the consumption which the government project would give rise to, since that is to be added to the benefit side of the calculation. Here our only interest is the cost of the project. Of course, in general,

$$C_t' < C_t \quad t = 0, 1, \ldots, T.$$

The real cost to society, then, is the difference in the two time streams. The present value of this difference is the social opportunity cost of the capital (SOCC) transferred to the public sector:

$$\text{SOCC} = \sum_{t=0}^{T} \frac{(C_t - C_t')}{(1 + d)^t}.$$

As suggested above, the practical approach to determining the SOCC is based on finding a multiplier to apply to the dollar costs of the project, rather than attempting to estimate the two consumption time streams. We use the following notation:

d is the social discount rate,

r is the marginal productivity of investment in the private sector, that is, r is the returns on \$1 invested in the private sector, and

θ is the amount of private investment displaced by each dollar of public investment.

For simplicity, we assume that the benefits of the investment projects are consumed as soon as they are made available and that investment projects earn r indefinitely. An example will clarify the approach. Let $d = .05$, $r = .15$, and $\theta = .1$. Consider the opportunity cost of investing \$1 in the public sector. Owing to the value of θ, we know that as the government taxes \$1 away from the private sector, \$.10 less private investment takes place, and consequently, there is \$.90 less consumption. Therefore, society initially pays a cost of \$.90 in foregone consumption. In addition, the \$.10 of foregone investment would have generated a future stream of benefits at the rate $r = .15$ per year. That is, $\$.10 \times .15 = \$.015$ worth of consumption is foregone in each succeeding year. However, because society has a positive social discount rate, future annual consumption payoffs of $\$.015$ must be discounted. The present value of that stream is

$$\frac{.015}{1.05} + \frac{.015}{(1.05)^2} + \frac{.015}{(1.05)^3} + \cdots = \frac{.015}{.05}$$

$$= .3$$

Thus, the opportunity cost of the $1 public investment is $\$.90$ in current consumption plus a stream of future consumption with the present value of .3, for a total of $1.20. In this case, the multiplier is 1.2, since 1.2 times the capital cost of the project ($1.00) equals $1.20. In general,

$$M = \theta \frac{r}{d} + (1 - \theta).$$

The first term on the right-hand side is the present value of the foregoing future consumption stream, whereas the second term represents the foregone present consumption.[12] The SOCC concept may be employed in a CBA by computing the present value of the benefits, PV(B), of the project (using the social discount rate) and subtracting the SOCC from this value. In general, SOCC would have to be computed for the capital invested in each year of the project.

Now, what can be said about the validity of this approach, and should it be adopted in CBA? First, we must state that its approach to the measurement of costs—the value of foregone

---

[12] The derivation of the closed form expression $\theta r/d$ from the infinite series is accomplished by noting that for any b, $0 < b < 1$,

$$\sum_{i=1}^{\infty} b^i = \frac{b}{1-b}.$$

Let $b = 1/(1 + d)$; we have

$$\sum_{i=1}^{\infty} \frac{\theta r}{(1 + d)^i} = \theta r \sum_{i=1}^{\infty} \frac{1}{(1 + d)^i} = \theta r \sum_{i=1}^{\infty} \left(\frac{1}{1 + d}\right)^i = \theta r \left(\frac{1}{1 + d}\right) \Big/ \left(1 - \frac{1}{1 + d}\right) = \frac{\theta r}{d}.$$

consumption—is unassailable. This is the approach stressed throughout this volume. A social cost is a benefit foregone. The real flaw of this approach is that it is built on questionable assumptions. When the assumptions are satisfied, the approach is valid. However, it is difficult to accept that the assumptions are generally satisfied to a degree sufficient to warrant the use of this approach. There are three basic assumptions involved. The first is the most unrealistic. It alone would be sufficient reason to preclude the general use of a SOCC multiplier in CBA.

ASSUMPTION 1

A government decision to implement a project causes a transfer of funds from the private sector to the public sector equal to the cost of the project.

The government budgetary process is an immensely complicated affair, and this is not the place to delve into how projects are financed. However, it is very definitely the case that it does *not* work such that the approval of a 1-million-dollar project at the agency level causes a memo to be sent to the Treasury specifying that an additional $1 M must be raised from the private sector. The $1 M comes out of the budget of the agency. There is no reason to believe this budget is any higher *because* of that specific project. If that project did not exist, another one would. Each agency vies for as large a budget as possible. The current appropriation of each agency is determined in large measure by its previous appropriation, current government fiscal and monetary policy, and the goals of the administration. Thus, a specific project may have little or no effect on the size of the allocated budget. Furthermore, since the size of the total government budget is dictated, at the margin, by broad economic policy objectives, more for one agency necessarily means less for another. What all this amounts to is that a project is in direct competition for funds with alternative projects of the same agency and indirectly with projects of other agencies. Thus, the base of reference for the analysis of a project should be the alternative use of funds within the government sector, not funds within the private sector.

ASSUMPTION 2

The transfer of funds from the private sector to the public sector reduces private investment.

While we have no quarrel with this assumption when taken literally, we must ask whether the transfer of funds causes a "significant" reduction in investment. If the true reduction is small, errors of measurement are likely to overwhelm the object of the measurement. It seems that this assumption ignores the "liquidity preference" aspects of economic behavior. For example, an increase in government taxation or borrowing could cause individuals to draw on their financial assets rather than forego investment opportunities. Even in a full-employment economy, consumption may decline in compensation for the transfer of purchasing power, and investment may not be affected.

ASSUMPTION 3

The foregone private investment has a time stream of impacts, the present value of which is positive.

This is a reasonable assumption; our objection is simply a way of introducing mitigating factors. First, private investment often has some negative side effects (external diseconomies) such as pollution. This tends to reduce its "face value." Second, the number of business failures indicates that much private investment is done in error. When a firm invests in an already saturated market, for example, it draws capital from other uses (a social cost), but the corporation may not survive to expand the amount of consumption goods available to the economy (no social benefit). However, since the effects we are discussing are marginal changes in total private investment, and businesses that fail are very likely to be well represented at this margin, a marginal decrease in total private investment may well reduce more than proportionately the number of "wrong" private investments. Again, the marginal social value of marginal private investment may be well below the average social value of private investments. This is an important point because, in practice, average values are often taken as proxies for marginal values.

The lack of faith in these three premises, particularly the first, has spurred an apparent consensus among economists that the social cost of a project should *not* be calculated using the multiplier approach (except, of course, in the unusual circumstance when the assumptions do appear satisfied).

6.4 FEDERAL GOVERNMENT DISCOUNTING PROCEDURE

The federal government currently has two distinct policies in effect regarding the choice of discount rates to be used in CBA. One policy is limited in application to water resource-related projects, whereas the other policy applies to all remaining projects.

The discounting procedure applicable to water related projects is explained in "Principles, Standards, and Procedures for Water and Related Land Resource Planning":

> The discount rate will be established in accordance with the concept that the Government's investment decisions are related to the cost of Federal borrowing.
>
> (a) The interest rate to be used in plan formulation and evaluation for discounting future benefits and costs, or otherwise converting benefits and costs to a common time basis, shall be based upon the estimated average cost of Federal borrowing as determined by the Secretary of the Treasury taking into consideration the average yield during the twelve months preceding his determination on interest-bearing marketable securities of the United States with remaining periods to maturity comparable to a 50-year period of investment: Provided, however, that the rate shall be raised or lowered by no

more than or less than one-half percentage point for any year.

When the average cost of Federal borrowing as determined by the Secretary of the Treasury exceeds the established discount rate by more than 0.25 percentage points, the rate shall be raised 0.5 percentage points. When the average cost is less than the established rate by more than 0.25 percentage points, the rate shall be lowered 0.5 percentage points.

(b) The Water Resources Council shall determine, as of July 1, the discount rate to be used during the fiscal year. The Director of the Water Resources Council shall annually request the Secretary of the Treasury during the month of June to advise the Water Resources Council of his determination of the average cost of Federal borrowing during the preceding twelve months.

(c) Notwithstanding the provisions of paragraphs (a) and (b) of this section, the discount rate to be used in plan formulation and evaluation during the remainder of the fiscal year 1974 shall be $6\frac{7}{8}$ percent. (U.S. Water Resources Council, 1973, p. 86)

While specifically exempting projects covered by the Water Resources Principles and Standards, Circular No. A-94 of the Office of Management and Budget (1972)

. . . applies to all agencies of the executive branch of the Federal Government except the U.S. Postal Service. The discount rate prescribed in the circular applies to the evaluation of government decisions concerning the initiation, renewal or expansion of all programs or projects, other than. . . (a few exceptions are noted), for which the adoption is expected to commit the government to a series of measurable costs extending over three or more years or which result in a series of benefits that extend three or more years beyond the inception date.

Further, OMB declares that the prescribed discount rates are

(1) Suggested for use in the internal planning documents of the agencies in the executive branch;
(2) Required for use in program analyses submitted to the Office of Management and Budget in support of legislative and budget programs. (p. 2)

In establishing its policy on the treatment of inflation, the Office of Management and Budget (1972) states:

All estimates of the costs and benefits for each year of the planning period should be made in constant dollars; i.e., in terms of the general purchasing power of the dollar at the time of decision. Estimates may reflect changes in the relative prices of cost and/or benefit components, where there is a reasonable basis for estimating such changes, but should not include any forecasted change in the general price level during the planning period. (p. 3)

Finally, the Office of Management and Budget (1972) sets its discount rate policy in the following terms:

The discount rates to be used for evaluations of programs and projects subject to the guidance of this Circular are as follows:
a. a rate of 10 percent; and, where relevant,
b. any other rate prescribed by or pursuant to law, Executive order, or other relevant Circulars.

The prescribed discount rate of 10 percent represents an estimate of the average rate of return on private investment, before taxes and after inflation. (p. 4)

Note the striking philosophical differences between these two approaches. The first approach, based on the federal cost of borrowing, is a risk-free, tax-free rate. The second approach, based on the returns to private investment, resembles the rate discussed in Section 6.3.3, "The Argument for a High Social Discount Rate." As the reader will recall from that discussion, the rate used by private (corporate) investors can be expressed as

[the government borrowing rate + a risk premium]

$$\times \left[\frac{1}{1 - \text{tax rate on profits}} \right]$$

For example, if the government borrowing rate is 6%, the risk premium is 2%, and the tax rate is 50%, then the private discount rate is 16%. If the tax rate were 30%, the private discount rate would be 11.4%. While the 10% rate mandated by the Office of Management and Budget is somewhat less than corporate discount rate calculations would suggest, it nonetheless embodies a totally different principle of discounting.

It is worth noting that the simultaneous use of two different discount rates in evaluating federal projects is a direct violation of conditions for efficient resource allocation. This assertion may be demonstrated with the aid of a simple model. Assume that the federal government invests in two broad categories of projects, for example, water resources and "everything else." Let I_1 and I_2 denote the number of dollars invested in each category. Clearly, I_1 and I_2 depend on the discount rate used in each category. Specifically, *ceteris paribus*, the lower the discount rate, the greater the investment. This is illustrated in Figure 6.3. At any one time there exists a number of investment opportunities with various rates of return. If the discount rate used in CBA is $\bar{r}_2$ for Category 2, then all investment projects with an internal rate of return greater than $\bar{r}_2$ will have a positive net present value, and will be undertaken. The total amount of investment in Category 2 will be $\bar{I}_2$, and the last dollar invested (the marginal investment) will have a return of $(1 + \bar{r}_2)$ dollars. Efficiency in resource allocation dictates that the maximum benefits should be extracted for any given level of total investment. Let $B_i(I_i)$ be a function relating the dollar value of benefits to the dollars invested for $i = 1, 2$. Let $\bar{I}$ be the total investment funds available. Then efficiency

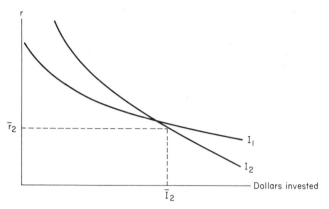

Figure 6.3   Investment and the discount rate.

means that we must

MAXIMIZE $B_1(I_1) + B_2(I_2)$

SUBJECT TO $I_1 + I_2 = \bar{I}.$

As shown by Figure 6.3, there is a relationship between I_i and the discount rate used. Denote these relationships as

$$I_1 = I_1(r_1)$$

and

$$I_2 = I_2(r_2).$$

Substituting these relationships into the problem, the relevant Lagrangian expression becomes

$$L = B_1[I_1(r_1)] + B_2[I_2(r_2)] + \lambda[\bar{I} - I_1(r_1) - I_2(r_2)].$$

First-order conditions include

$$\frac{\partial B_1}{\partial I_1}\frac{\partial I_1}{\partial r_1} - \lambda\frac{\partial I_1}{\partial r_1} = 0,$$

$$\frac{\partial B_2}{\partial I_2}\frac{\partial I_2}{\partial r_2} - \lambda\frac{\partial I_2}{\partial r_2} = 0.$$

Solving each condition for the Langrangian multiplier λ and equating yields

$$\frac{\partial B_1}{\partial I_1} = \frac{\partial B_2}{\partial I_2}.$$

Now $\partial B_i/\partial I_i$ is the benefit from the marginal dollar invested in projects in Category i. This value was identified above as $(1 + \bar{r}_i)$. Thus, the foregoing conditions translate to

$$(1 + \bar{r}_1) = (1 + \bar{r}_2),$$

or, of course, $\bar{r}_1 = \bar{r}_2$. We see that a necessary condition for maximizing the benefits from different categories of investments is that the same discount rate must be used in evaluating all projects. Upon reflection, this result is intuitively appealing. Whenever a discrepancy in the rates exists, resources can be withdrawn from the category earning the lower rate and invested in the category with the higher rate, resulting in a net increase in benefits. In the case of current government decision making, the result suggests that resources used in marginally acceptable water resources programs could have a greater payoff in other areas.

6.5 CHOOSING A DISCOUNT RATE

Finally, we must get down to the basic question: What is the cost-benefit analyst to do about the discount rate? Which rate should be employed? While this chapter hopefully has illuminated some of the implications of and rationales for various rates, it has not prescribed an unswerving course for the analyst to follow. As might be expected with so complicated an issue, no such single best approach has yet been devised. Nonetheless, all is not lost.

First, it must be borne in mind that the issues discussed in this chapter are in the realm of the welfare-theoretic foundations of cost-benefit. In the application of CBA to the evaluation of a project, little explicit attention is typically accorded to the theoretical foundations of the chosen discounting procedure. This is as it should be. Economists have devoted scores, perhaps hundreds, of man-years to investigating the discounting issue. It is unlikely that significant progress would be made in the confines of a single applied project, yet it is likely that research into the discounting issue would quickly expend project funds best put to other uses. We feel very strongly that cost–benefit analysts should be aware of and familiar with the nuances of discounting, but at the same time the research program—the actual CBA—is not the place to further research aimed at finding the true social discount rate.

One of three situations usually prevails regarding the choice of the discount in a CBA. First, the rate to be employed is dictated exogeneously. This might prevail if the project fell under the authority of Circular A-94 of the Office of Management and Budget or the Water Resources Council (1973) in "Principles for Planning." Whether agreeing or disagreeing with the mandated discounting rule, the analyst has no alternative but to comply with procedures in the context of the project. In the second case, there is no externally imposed discount rate, but the decision maker has strong feelings about the appropriate one to use. Here, the analyst's familiarity with the underlying issues and ramifications, as touched upon in this chapter, comes to the fore. It is the analyst's task to interact with the decision maker in examining underlying concepts and specific rates. The effort must always be directed toward improving the quality of the decision process.

When there is some uncertainty about the rate to be employed, a computation of the *critical rate* is sometimes helpful. The critical discount rate is that rate at which NPV of the project being considered changes sign. If the critical rate is either sufficiently high or sufficiently low, the analyst is spared the agony of setting a single best discount rate. Suppose that the critical rate is 15%, and NPV > 0 for any rate less than 15%; the decision maker and analyst might then agree jointly that, while they do not have great confidence in any particular rate, the proper rate is surely less than 15%, and the project is worth pursuing.

Table 6.1 will enable the reader to get a "feel" for alternative discount rates. The entries in the table are the "weights" as-

TABLE 6.1
Effective Discounting Weights

Discount rate	N:	Weight in Nth year				
		5	10	20	30	40
0		1.0	1.0	1.0	1.0	1.0
1		.95	.90	.82	.74	.67
3		.86	.74	.55	.41	.30
5		.78	.61	.38	.23	.14
7		.71	.51	.26	.13	.07
10		.62	.39	.15	.06	.02
15		.50	.25	.06	.02	.00

signed through the discounting process to costs or benefits incurred in the corresponding year and at the corresponding discount rate. For example, at a discount rate of 7%, a benefit incurred 20 years into the future is worth only 26% of what the same benefit would be worth if it were incurred in the present. The data in the table suggest that one might choose a discount rate by first deciding on weights for the various years, and then choosing the best corresponding discount rate.

6.6 SUMMARY

In this chapter we dealt with some of the theoretical and practical difficulties surrounding the discount rate issue in CBA. Perhaps the most important point is that *the rate matters*. Experience has shown that cost–benefit results are generally quite sensitive to the discount rate.

Experts disagree on both the proper numerical value of the discount rate and its conceptual foundation. Some argue for adoption of the social rate of time preference as the conceptual foundation, and, concomitantly, a discount rate below market rates. Others espouse the social opportunity cost of capital as the conceptual basis, and a correspondingly high rate.

The Federal Government has adopted an apparently schizophrenic stance on this matter. Two rates are employed—one for water related projects and one for all others. Currently, these rates are approximately 7% and 10%, respectively.

When the cost-benefit analyst is uncertain regarding the appropriate discount rate, a sensitivity analysis usually proves helpful. This analysis determines how critical the discount rate really is in the project at hand. Sensitivity analysis is the subject of Chapter 8.

7
SOCIAL AND ENVIRONMENTAL IMPACT ANALYSIS

To define it rudely but not inaptly, engineering is the art of doing that well with one dollar which any bungler can do with two after a fashion.

Arthur M. Wellington, *The Economic Theory of Railway Location:*
Introduction

7.1 INTRODUCTION

A major problem in the appraisal of public projects has been the fragmentation of analyses into partial statements covering "economic" and "social," and "environmental" impacts. Depending upon which influence groups are dominant, project analyses have included such impact statements in various degrees of completeness. We believe this fragmentation to be in error, and we feel that a properly defined cost–benefit analysis would be addressed to a review of *all* costs and *all* benefits. Nevertheless, we would be remiss if we did not at least note some of the special problems associated with social and environmental impacts.

The field is now so cluttered with definitions that it is almost improper to attempt a precise definition of terms. However, we could generally say that *economic impacts* refer to effects on the "national economic development" objective. These effects lead to changes in the value of the output of goods and services and changes in national economic efficiency. *Social impacts* are effects on the distribution of income as well as on the psychological, social, and physical well-being of individuals affected by a project. Finally, *environmental impacts* result in changes in our physical and biological surroundings as they are perceived to effect the quality of life. Actually, these distinctions are arbitrary. In the end, almost all relevant effects of projects are social. The economic or environmental consequences of a project are ultimately interpreted by their effects on social well-being. The term *social cost–benefit analysis*, here abbreviated to *cost–benefit analysis*, properly focuses our interests.

In the remainder of this chapter we very briefly examine both social and environmental impact analysis as subsets of our interests.

7.2 SOCIAL IMPACT ANALYSIS

Social impact analysis originated in a need to insure that a CBA presenting only the costs and benefits which can be given a dollar valuation not be taken as encompassing all effects of a project. To a perceptive analyst or to a person accustomed to reviewing good analyses, introduction of a new term was unnecessary. What was and is needed is simply a correct interpretation of the analyst's task to begin with. Nevertheless, the term has taken its place in our vocabulary in response to shortcomings appearing in existing analyses.

Most of the problems relating to the term "social impact analysis" are measurement problems. As discussed in Section 3.2, some effects, called "incommensurables and intangibles," are difficult both to identify and to measure. The former are effects that are not readily measured in monetary terms. With those, the problem is not so much determining whether the effect is good or bad, but what magnitude ought to be attached to it. The latter are noneconomic effects and so not only are not measurable in dollars but defy any measurement whatsoever. In general, these effects must be judged by values beyond economic ones.

Examples of incommensurables are recreation, nonrenewable resources, and changes in technology. Intangibles may relate to politics, some demographic effects, social justice, individual liberty, aesthetics, and social harmony. The reader is referred back to Section 3.2.3 for further discussion.

A second problem leading to the use of the term "social impact analysis" is associated with the regional effects of a project. The problem is really one of definition.

If the economy under study is that of the region itself, the regional effects of the projects are the economic effects—the benefits and costs—themselves, and no problem exists. If the economy under study is that of the nation, then the regional development effects may or may not be subject to inclusion in project evaluation. Under conditions of full employment, resources employed in a project in one region have been diverted from use in others. In this case, the regional benefits and costs should clearly be counted, and the problem is no different from the usual CBA problem. Under conditions of severe resource unemployment, the unemployed resources may be used at no cost to society. Accounting for these resources as costless over any length of time, however, requires such strong assumptions about the future that the general concensus of opinion is to account for resources at normal market costs and to avoid "full employment" as a potential benefit.

Other problems leading to the use of the term "social impact analysis" are concerned primarily with the definition of objectives. If the objective of a project is solely national efficiency, then the distributional changes pursued in a social impact analysis are superfluous. As noted in Section 3.2.4, the indirect effects of a project on regional development, or on a regional redistribution of resource use under conditions of full employment, and the effects of a project on the distribution of income among classes are effects that are to be included in a calculation of costs and benefits subject to some specific assumptions. If, as is traditional, the *net* gain "to whomsoever it may accrue" is a primary concern, redistributions may represent double counting. If the objective of a project is to effect a redistribution of the total product (broadly defined) of that society across income classes, regions, or other groupings of the population, however, then the objective function of the CBA for this project must be similarly defined.

As mentioned above, in any cost–benefit analysis certain of the identified effects of a project will be incommensurable or intangible. That is, they will not readily lend themselves to quantification or monetary valuation. The problem, of course, is that such effects, nonetheless, must be somehow incorporated in the cost–benefit analysis. Social effects are no less costs or benefits because of their inherent intractability. As a decision *aid*, the CBA must present all relevant information to the decision maker.

7.3 ENVIRONMENTAL IMPACT ANALYSIS

Environmental impact analysis originated with continued neglect of the environmental consequences of public projects. Increasing concern in the United States eventually forced the passage of the National Environmental Policy Act (NEPA) in 1969. This act requires that an environmental impact statement (EIS) be prepared for any "major federal projects likely to have significant effects on the human environment." It is not our purpose here to discuss the guidelines established by the Council on Environmental Quality or to comment on the specific regulations developed by individual Federal agencies for use in preparing their own EISs. Rather, we would like to repeat our continued emphasis on the all-inclusive nature of a good cost–benefit analysis and to discuss only briefly some of the problems associated with environmental impact analysis.

Four problems are acute in this part of cost–benefit analysis: the criteria or political problem, the identification problem, the measurement problem, and the presentation problem.

Politically, the primary problem is determining the environmental objective function. This function cannot be specified easily, and usually can be identified only after the fact. This difficulty arises principally because of the incommensurable nature of environmental goods and bads. Since they seldom can be valued or quantified in terms appropriate for comparisons, the decision maker must weigh them politically.

For each project and situation as well as for society, however, we must evolve a set of environmental objectives. How do we balance the clamor of the pure conservationists for a steady-state economy against the demands of consumers for an increasing production of goods and services? How do we preserve our cultural heritage, correct our environmental oversights, lay a sound foundation for the future? How do we satisfy our Biblical charge to ". . . be fruitful and multiply, and replenish the earth, and subdue it: and have dominion over the fish of the sea, and over the fowl of the air, and over every living thing that moveth upon the earth" (Gen. 1:28)?

The decision problem is so overwhelming that our political leaders must rely heavily on the identification by analysts of the environmental consequences. Here the question is one of perception and of proper identification and measurement of long-term biological and economic effects.

The most serious question pertains to identifying stock pollutants and to the impact of nonreducible pollutants on society. Examples of accumulations that have been identified after it is too late are mercury, PCB, cadmium, and other chemical concentrations. In the case of cadmium, for example, this substance has accumulated unnoticed in human bodies via food and water ingestions, and its severely damaging effects were perceived only after the fact. The so-called "itai-itai" disease among certain Japanese citizens was a result of such unperceived pollution (see Pearce, 1976). The "gunk" content of dredgings from Great Lakes ports is another example. Industrial wastes are now so concentrated in the dredgings in Toronto that these dredgings cannot be placed on cultivatable lands, and disposal has become a serious nuisance, with estimated costs now much higher than the costs of pollution control. The problem might have been alleviated by proper regulations, but the need for such regulations has only been recently perceived.

Measurement of environmental impacts is, as noted above, especially difficult. Some impacts, such as aesthetic ones, cannot be measured even in their own terms, whereas others, such as pollutant concentrations in streams, can be measured but valuation in dollar terms is not possible. In fact, if we lay aside the question of perceiving subtle and irreversible pollutant buildups, their measurement becomes the most difficult problem in environmental analysis. The market provides little assistance, for environmental quality has not been for private sale. While we can ask people to state the value of various scenarios, the answers are likely to be meaningless. We cannot ask people to value what they have never paid for: people say one thing and believe another, especially when they understand the purpose of a questionnaire; propaganda might undermine consumer sovereignty either way on a given question, and the worth of a citizen's evaluation of a project depends on knowledge of alternatives and consequences, knowledge that is frequently if not always missing for environmental questions.

All of these problems—decision, identification, and measurement—lead to a final question of presentation. How do you organize a massive set of facts and opinions for easy review by critics and decision makers? Patterns differ by agencies, but the following may be a typical outline:

(1) Description of the project, including background, site considerations, operation, maintenance, termination plans, and abandonment plans.

(2) Description of the environment, including land, water

and air quality; natural species; socioeconomic characteristics, including population, cultural characteristics,
business and industrial activity, and other relevant
economic features; and unique features such as archeo-
logical and historical sites, parks, refuges, and biologi-
cally sensitive areas.

(3) Environmental impact of proposed project, including
     site preparation and construction, water and air quality,
     species and ecosystem changes, waste disposal, socioec-
     onomic effects, and the potential effects of accidents and
     natural disasters.

(4) Probable unavoidable adverse environmental effects.

(5) Relation between short-term and long-term effects of
     the project.

(6) Irreversible or irretrievable commitment of resources.

(7) Alternatives to proposed project.

(8) Relation to land-use plans.

(9) Consultations and comments by interested parties.

The list, obviously, can vary with project. Also, depending on
the overall framework for the cost–benefit analysis, the environmental statement may emphasize certain points and may overlap
significantly with both the social impact analysis and the economic analysis.

7.4 SUMMARY

Let us summarize with a few comments on what an impact
analysis should do and be. First, it should provide a broad
representation of the concerns of special interest groups and how
they interact. This representation may come from harsh and
critical reviews by the interest groups themselves, or it may come
from the balanced approach of an analyst who is aware of the
implications of his study. The distribution of costs and benefits
is an important element of social impact analysis. Second, it

should produce a manageable set of decision indicators, whether quantified or narrative. A lengthy compilation of statistics without interpretation is hardly an adequate basis for a decision. Third, scenarios for the various alternative projects to achieve a proposed goal must be reviewed to show the options open in both the present and the future for use of public resources. And fourth, the terminology of the final decision document must be understandable to the general public.

Social and environmental impact analyses treat a variety of problems associated with the proper identification of project objectives and the measurement of project effects. Such analyses arose from a feeling that cost-benefit analyses were incomplete, focusing only on effects measurable in dollars. As defined here, however, cost-benefit analysis is all-inclusive, attempting to ferret out the true costs and benefits of public projects, regardless of categorization.

8
SENSITIVITY ANALYSIS

Chance favors the prepared mind.

Louis Pasteur

8.1 INTRODUCTION

Up to this point, emphasis has been placed on the identification and measurement of specific costs and benefits as they relate to CBA. Of course, any CBA will involve the consideration of a number of different costs and a number of different benefits, each spanning a number of years. We know, from Chapter 2, that the best way to aggregate these figures into a single number useful for decision making is to compute the net present value of a project.

If b_{it} is the value of the ith benefit received in year t, and c_{it} is the value of the ith cost paid in year t, the expression for net present value (NPV) is

$$\text{NPV} = \sum_t \frac{\sum_i b_{it} - \sum_i c_{it}}{(1 + d)^t}.$$

For example, b_{it} might be the value to all consumers of a drop in the price of some good for some year, and c_{it} might be the value to all consumers of an increase in pollution for that year. In previous sections it was pointed out how the b_{it}'s and the c_{it}'s should be estimated, the correct measurement approach depending on the specific circumstances.

Of course, each b_{it} and c_{it} that is estimated will be just that—an estimate. Clearly, the reliability of the final NPV figure will depend on the accuracy of these estimates. Admonishing the analyst to be accurate does not resolve the issue of NPV reliability, for there is always some degree of error inherent to the measurement process itself. Even if one attempts to measure a physical phenomenon which occurred in the past, say, the change in wheat production from 1973 to 1974, one can never be completely accurate. In CBA, many of the measurements deal with the nonphysical, such as willingness to pay, and all deal with the future and thus are predictions. No one is likely to accept, under these circumstances, that the calculated NPV of a project is to be interpreted as a precise figure. Given the intrinsic uncertainty surrounding the computed NPV, is there any way the analyst can aid the decision maker, beyond the perfunctory caveat that the computations are subject to error? The answer, of course, is positive. The analyst should provide the decision maker with some idea of the degree of error to which the estimates are subject. Then, for example, in a CBA of two alternative projects, if the NPV estimate of one is "much" larger than the NPV estimate of the other, and the analyst finds that the degree of error is "small," the decision maker can feel confident about the choice of the former over the latter. On the other hand, if the difference in the estimates of NPV were small relative to the degree of error, the decision maker might well choose the other, or neither, or commission a CBA of a third project, a further study of the original two, etc.

The important point is that the analyst should present to the decision maker as much information as possible in a format useful to the decision maker. The analyst must be careful to imply neither a greater nor lesser degree of confidence in this estimate than the data permit.

The reader will recognize that, to some extent, we are saying that the variance of an estimate should supplement the mean as input to the decision-making process. In contrast, the argument is often made that for public projects the mean alone is a sufficient decision input. This argument rests on the premise that, at any given time, the government is engaged in a large number of similarly risky projects. Those that fail to meet expectations are balanced out by those that more than do so. Thus, the deviations cancel out, and society ends up with the mean values. The argument is theoretically sound, given the premise. However, there is no evidence that this premise is usually satisfied. It is quite to the contrary, and experience would suggest that each project has a number of unique characteristics. The acceptance of the mean alone as a decision guideline is not appropriate, as a general rule. In our discussion below, it is assumed that some measure of dispersion is relevant to the decision.

The analyst's attempts to gauge the degree of error in his estimates fall under the general term *sensitivity analysis*. Conceptually, we can distinguish among three levels of sensitivity analysis: subjective estimates, selective sensitivity analysis, and general sensitivity analysis. In the following sections these levels are discussed in detail.

8.2 SUBJECTIVE ESTIMATES

This is the least rigorous and quickest approach. Calling on previous experience, intuition, "gut feeling," and the like, the analyst determines some estimate of the actual degree of error. For example, after calculating the NPV of a project, the analyst might state that this figure is subject to an error of plus or minus 10%, or that the chance of the true NPV being more than 10% different from the estimate is less than 1 in 20. There are any number of ways the analyst can state an error estimate. However, the point here is that the error estimate is obtained subjectively, that is, without recourse to formal calculation.

Depending on the skill of the analyst, a subjective error estimate may well be quite good. The advantages of subjective estimates are the fact that they can account for variability not reflected in objective measures, and (ordinarily) the speed with which they can be formulated. The drawbacks of the subjective approach are that the decision maker may place less confidence in such an estimate and that he may have difficulty in defending his decision to critics. Further, the absence of a well-defined approach to error determination, which necessarily occurs in subjective estimates, makes it impossible for anyone to trace the analyst's approach and to assess its reasonableness.

8.3   SELECTIVE SENSITIVITY ANALYSIS

This is an objective approach to error estimation in the sense that it is arrived at via an explicit series of calculations. The most common variant of selective sensitivity analysis goes as follows. The analyst selects a parameter in the NPV calculation that he feels is both subject to error and capable of significantly affecting the NPV calculation. The analyst selects likely high and low (or best and worst) values for this parameter and computes the NPV with each. The decision maker is then presented with three NPV estimates for each project—high, medium, and low—and for each parameter selected for sensitivity analysis.

For example, in a project to determine the economic viability of a wind energy system, the price of oil for the period 1980–1985 may be an important parameter. The NPV for the project would be computed initially by using all the "best" estimates for each parameter. Then, NPV would be computed, using the high and low prices of oil, but retaining the same "best" estimates of other parameters. Thus, the decision maker will have information on how sensitive NPV is to the 1980–1985 price of oil. The same procedure, for example, could be carried out for the 1980–1985 demand for electricity, or the discount rate.

The advantages of selective sensitivity analysis derive from its objective nature and relative ease of computation. Its objectivity ensures that defenders and critics alike argue the merits of the analysis on well-specified data and assumptions. The major difficulty with this approach is that it is usually unsuited for the analysis of anything more than a few parameters. This difficulty can be appreciated from the following.

For concreteness, let us suppose that the calculations for each of two alternative projects involve 10 parameters, each a candidate for sensitivity analysis. A selective sensitivity analyses on the 10 parameters would produce 20 NPVs for each project, in addition to the initial "best" estimate. The analyst must present to the decision maker a total of 42 NPVs. Such a large number of figures may not aid the decision maker at all. In fact, the presentation of all NPV estimates might even violate the analyst's charge to present the decision maker with results in a format *convenient* for use.

Even more important than format convenience, the 21 NPVs presented to the decision maker for each project omit a great deal of important information. For instance, the decision maker may well wish to know the worst outcome that can reasonably be expected. He might associate this outcome with the *simultaneous* realization of, say, seven worst outcomes and three medium outcomes on the parameters. (Recall that this information is not computed under selective sensitivity analysis. Each parameter is evaluated at its worst while every other parameter is set at medium. No simultaneous "worsts" are calculated.) Furthermore, the decision maker would undoubtedly like to know the chance of such a "worst" outcome.

The reader may object that it is not difficult, in principle, to calculate all the combinations of worst, medium, and best on each parameter. True. Then, for this relatively simple case of 10 parameters, we would be presenting the decision maker with 3^{10}, or 59,049, NPVs for each project! And we still have not incorporated information such as the *chance* of one of the bottom 1000 outcomes actually happening. These objections are all answered by the next approach.

8.4 GENERAL SENSITIVITY ANALYSIS

8.4.1 Problem Formulation

This approach hinges on the derivation of a *probability distribution* of NPV outcomes. In this way, all of the information contained in the 59,049 individual possible NPV outcomes of the previous paragraph is captured in a format very convenient for the decision maker. For each project, the decision maker can tell at a glance what are the chances of breaking even, of complete disaster, or of overwhelming triumph. Since the approach is likely to be least familiar to the reader, we shall sketch it in greater detail than the previous approaches.

The b_{it} and the c_{it} that constitute the heart of the NPV calculation depend, in general, on a number of factors, or parameters. Call these parameters the set

$$\alpha = \{\alpha_1, \alpha_2, \ldots, \alpha_K\}.$$

For each specification of α, a particular NPV will result.

Now, in general, the members of α will not all be independent of each other. For example, suppose α contains the following three parameters:

(a) 1985 price of oil P_O,
(b) 1985 quantity of oil consumed Q_O, and
(c) 1985 price of natural gas P_G.

Suppose further that high, medium, and low estimates are available for each. These high, medium, and low estimates are

TABLE 8.1
Illustrative Occurrence Probabilities

	Probability of occurence		
Parameter	High	Medium	Low
P_0	1/3	1/2	1/6
Q_0	1/6	1/2	1/3
P_G	1/3	1/2	1/6

projected to occur with certain probabilities for each parameter. Table 8.1 summarizes the nature of the raw data. Since these are three parameters, each with three possible values, it might be thought that these parameters alone would give rise to 3^3 or 27 NPV figures (for each specification of the remaining parameters in α_j). This would not be correct. Since these three parameters are related, only *certain* of the 27 possibilities can really occur. The relation is clear from elementary economic reasoning. The price of oil and the quantity consumed are related by the demand curve for oil. The higher the price, the lower the quantity; and conversely. Figure 8.1 depicts the necessary relation. It is clear that, rather than nine possible combinations of values for P_0 and

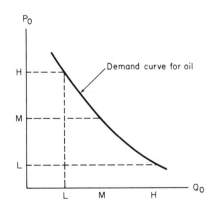

Figure 8.1   Illustrative demand curve for oil.

Q_0, there are only three. These are

$$(P_0, Q_0) = (H, L), \quad (M, M), \quad (L, H).$$

In many ways, natural gas is a substitute for oil. Thus, if the price of oil were high, some users would switch to gas, increasing the demand for that product. The increased demand, of course, drives up the price of gas. The relation between the prices of oil and gas is illustrated in Figure 8.2. Here D_L, D_M, and D_H are the demand curves for gas when the price of oil is low, medium, and high, respectively. Note that the market price of natural gas will tend to be high, medium, or low as the market price of oil is high, medium, or low, respectively. Thus, there are only three, not nine, possible relations between P_0 and P_G. There are

$$(P_0, P_G) = (H, H), \quad (M, M), \quad (L, L).$$

Finally, it is clear that, instead of 27, there are only three possible sets of values for all three parameters:

$$(P_0, Q_0, P_G) = (H, L, H), \quad (M, M, M), \quad (L, H, L).$$

The associated probabilities are $\frac{1}{3}$, $\frac{1}{2}$, and $\frac{1}{6}$, respectively, for these sets to occur. Note how the proper consideration of dependencies among parameters *does* affect the final NPV probability distributions. As an example, if we proceeded as though the three parameters were not related, we would assign the outcome (H,

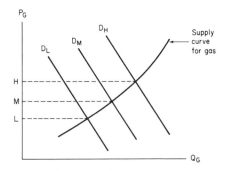

Figure 8.2 Illustrative demand and supply curves for gas, given various oil prices.

M, H) a probability of $\frac{1}{3} \times \frac{1}{2} \times \frac{1}{3} = \frac{1}{18}$, and a corresponding NPV would be calculated. In fact, (H, M, H) will not occur, and so its correct probability is zero, and no corresponding NPV is to be figured.

Let us now generalize this discussion and incorporate it into the scheme of general sensitivity analysis. The parameters in the set α must be separated into subsets on the following bases:

(a) If any two parameters α_i and α_j are related, they must be in the same subset.

(b) If any two parameters α_i and α_j are not related, they cannot be in the same subset.

It follows that each α_i must be a member of one, and only one, subset. (It is likely that some subsets have only one α_i in them.) Let us denote these subsets as A_1, A_2, . . . , A_j, . . . , A_J, where

$$A_j = \{\alpha_i, \ldots\}$$

and

$$J \leq K \quad \text{(the number of original parameters).}$$

Since the α_i's in each A_j are related, there are only certain combinations of values each A_j can assume. The analyst must determine these combinations and the corresponding probabilities. Suppose the set A_j can assume θ_j different configurations. Denote these configurations as

$$A_{j1}, \quad A_{j2}, \ldots, A_{j\theta_j},$$

and the corresponding probabilities as

$$P(A_{j1}), \quad P(A_{j2}), \ldots, PA_{j\theta_j}).$$

Naturally, the probabilities over the values of any A_j must sum to unity.

It might be useful at this point to summarize the discussion and clarify the notation with an example. Suppose

$$\alpha = \{\alpha_1, \alpha_2, \alpha_3, \alpha_4, \alpha_5, \alpha_6\},$$

and

$$A_1 = \{\alpha_1, \alpha_3, \alpha_4\},$$
$$A_2 = \{\alpha_2, \alpha_5\},$$
$$A_3 = \{\alpha_6\}.$$

Then we might have

$$A_{11} = (H, L, H),$$
$$A_{12} = (M, M, M),$$
$$A_{13} = (L, H, L);$$

$$A_{21} = (L, L),$$
$$A_{22} = (L, M),$$
$$A_{23} = (M, M),$$
$$A_{24} = (M, H);$$

$$A_{31} = (L),$$
$$A_{32} = (M),$$
$$A_{33} = (H);$$

and

$$P(A_{11}) = 1/3,$$
$$P(A_{12}) = 1/2,$$
$$P(A_{13}) = 1/6;$$

$$P(A_{21}) = 1/10,$$
$$P(A_{22}) = 3/10,$$
$$P(A_{23}) = 4/10,$$
$$P(A_{24}) = 2/10;$$

$$P(A_{31}) = 1/3,$$
$$P(A_{32}) = 1/3,$$
$$P(A_{33}) = 1/3.$$

In this example, we have

$$K = 6,$$
$$J = 3,$$
$$\theta_1 = 3,$$
$$\theta_2 = 4,$$
$$\theta_3 = 3.$$

Returning to our development of general sensitivity analysis, we are now prepared to derive the final distribution of NPV. This can be done in either of two ways: complete enumeration or random sampling.

8.4.2 Complete Enumeration

When the total number of parameter combinations ($\theta_1 \times \theta_2 \times \cdots \times \theta_J$) is small, say less than a few hundred, then all the possible NPVs can be computed, along with their corresponding probabilities. (The use of an electronic computer would certainly ease matters.) It should be clear to the reader that the number of NPV calculations equals the number of parameter combinations. Each calculation will yield a NPV and a probability of observing it. Of course, the probability is calculated separately from the NPV. In terms of the foregoing example, we might begin by choosing A_{11}, A_{21}, and A_{31}. This means we have parameter values:

$$(A_{11}, A_{21}, A_{31}) = (\alpha_1, \alpha_2, \alpha_3, \alpha_4, \alpha_5, \alpha_6)$$
$$= (H, L, L, H, L, L).$$

In practice, naturally, actual numbers replace the H's, M's, and L's. With all the parameters specified, the NPV is calculated—say, NPV = 1000. We then compute

$$P(A_{11}) \times P(A_{21}) \times P(A_{31}) = 1/90.$$

For the example, 36 (3 × 4 × 3) such calculations must be performed to yield all possible pairs of NPV and the corresponding probability. From these pairs, it is an easy matter to construct the cumulative probability density function of NPV for the project at hand. To do this, choose a number of arbitrary NPV figures, and add up the probabilities of the calculated NPVs that fall below each of those arbitrarily chosen figures. The results may be plotted to yield a graphical display. It would look something like Figure 8.3. The interpretation is straightforward. The decision maker can tell at a glance that, should he choose this project,

(a) The chance that its NPV turns out less than zero is about .05 or one in 20;
(b) there is no chance that it can lose more than 1000;
(c) the chance of a positive return is 95%;
(d) the chance of a return over 5000 is zero;
(e) the chance of a return between 0 and 3000 is about 80%;
(f) the expected (or best single estimate of) NPV is 1500.

Quite clearly, the NPV cumulative probability distribution is a powerful tool for the decision maker. With this tool the decision maker is presented with all the relevant information in a very convenient format and explicitly shown what risks a decision entails.

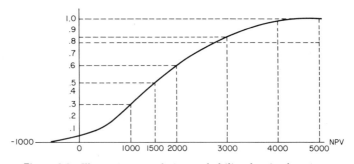

Figure 8.3   Illustrative cumulative probability density function.

8.4.3 Random Sampling

When the total number of parameter combinations ($\theta_1 \times \theta_2 \times \cdots \times \theta_J$) is large, it is both impractical and unnecessary to compute the NPV and associated probability for each combination. Instead, a random sample of, say, 1000 combinations can be drawn from the total population of combinations. The random process is assurance that these 1000 will be representative. The NPV cumulative probability function is then derived just as above. The interpretation is also the same as above.

8.5 RISK AND UNCERTAINTY

In our discussion of general sensitivity analysis, we have assumed that, somehow, the analyst is able to assign meaningful probabilities to the sets of α_i's, that is, to A_1, A_2, etc. Suppose that the analyst determines that for some subset of the α_i's, say, $A_{j1}, \ldots, A_{j\theta_j}$, he simply cannot assign probabilities that are anything more than totally arbitrary. Formally, this situation—in which meaningful probabilities cannot be assigned—is called a situation of *uncertainty*, whereas the situation in which probabilities are assignable is called a situation of *risk*. Thus, our previous discussion has dealt with risk, not uncertainty. It is difficult to say why probabilities can be assigned in one circumstance and not in another. To some extent, it is a matter of the analyst's judgment. However, it is probably fair to say that uncertain situations are usually relatively unique and/or involve guessing about conscious human choice. For example, an analyst might well consider that the state of East-West relations over Berlin in 1980 is an uncertain situation. However, the state of midwestern rainfall in 1980 is a risk environment: using past data, meaningful probabilities (albeit rough) can be assigned to the possible outcomes.

Does the uncertainty of a parameter—the inability or unwillingness of the analyst to assign probabilities to the possible values of that parameter—destroy general sensitivity analysis? No, but it does complicate matters somewhat. The analyst must now compute a NPV cumulative probability function *for each value* (say *H, M, L*) of the uncertain parameter, or set of parameters. In terms of the previous example, suppose that the analyst has *uncertainty* about the possible values of $A_1 = (\alpha_1, \alpha_3, \alpha_4)$. That is, the analyst knows the possible values are (H, L, H), (M, M, M), and (L, H, L), but cannot assign probabilities to these outcomes. Three NPV cumulative probability functions can be computed, each one taking one of the uncertain values as given. All this information is then presented to the decision maker, who must subjectively determine the likelihood of the occurrence of the uncertain states, and act accordingly. The important point is that the analyst has provided the decision maker with as much information as possible, in a digestable format. By admitting uncertainty, the analyst has not implied that his or her calculations are more precise than they really are.

8.6 CHOICE OF SENSITIVITY ANALYSIS

In the previous sections of this chapter we have described the three levels at which sensitivity analysis can be performed. Which one should the analyst use? If the cost–benefit analyst were not constrained by time and resources in conducting a CBA, general sensitivity analysis would be our recommendation for all but the simplest cases because it provides the most complete and reliable information in a digestable format for the decision maker. However, the time and resources available for a CBA are never unlimited. In the absence of a specific charge by the decision maker, the analyst must determine the proper level of sensitivity analysis by an exercise of judgment. Is there some rule to guide this judgment? Yes—the economic rule for efficient resource use in production, since the analyst is *producing* a good, the CBA. Suppose that the analyst determines that the CBA comprises five tasks:

(1) Defining the problem and specifying alternative approaches.
(2) Identifying relevant costs and benefits.
(3) Measuring costs and benefits.
(4) Sensitivity analysis.
(5) Preparing the final report.

The analyst is budgeted a certain amount of money M to perform the analysis. The analyst must decide how much money to allocate to the performance of each task. The rule that should be followed is: Distribute the money among the tasks so that the marginal dollar allocated to each task improves the overall CBA by the same amount.[1] To appreciate the sense of this rule, suppose that it is violated. Then, say, the marginal dollar used in Task 1 contributes three "units" of quality to the CBA while the marginal dollar used in Task 2 contributes five "units." This allocation is clearly suboptimal because, by switching one dollar from Task 1 to Task 2, the overall quality can be improved by two "units."

---

[1] Let $M_1, M_2, \ldots, M_5$ be the amounts allocated to each of the five tasks. Since M is the total amount available,

$$M = M_1 + M_2 + \cdots + M_5.$$

Let Z be an index of the overall quality of the CBA. Thus

$$Z = F(M_1, M_2, M_3, M_4, M_5).$$

The Lagrangian function is

$$L = F(M_1, M_2, M_3, M_4, M_5) + \lambda(M - M_1 - M_2 - M_3 - M_4 - M_5).$$

The necessary condition for $(M_1{}^*, M_2{}^*, \ldots, M_5{}^*)$ to be optimal allocations are given by differentiating L with respect to the six variables, the M_i's, and λ. The result is that $(M_1{}^*, M_2{}^*, \ldots, M_5{}^*)$ must satisfy

$$\frac{\partial F}{\partial M_1} = \frac{\partial F}{\partial M_2} = \cdots + \frac{\partial F}{\partial M_5}.$$

Thus, the return from the marginal dollar used in Task 1 must equal the return from the marginal dollar used in Task 2, etc.

We stress that this is a judgment issue for the analyst. Units of quality cannot be readily defined, and the marginal contribution of a dollar to this task or that is an imprecise notion at best. However, if the analyst must make the allocation decision, keeping the economic-efficiency rule in mind should aid that decision. Therefore, in deciding on a level of sensitivity analysis, the analyst must consider the demands of the decision maker, the necessary trade-offs among dollars spent on the various tasks, and how each task contributes to the overall CBA.

9

PERFORMING A
COST–BENEFIT ANALYSIS

Get your facts first, then you can distort them as much as you please.

Mark Twain

9.1 INTRODUCTION

The purpose of this chapter is to present an overall design for CBA and integrate the material of earlier chapters into that design. Our central theme of this section is the importance of planning the design, or charting the course, of a CBA. Too often, the tendency is to plunge directly into gathering data and estimating benefits and costs with the hope that it will all fit together at the end. In an undertaking as complex as CBA, this is not a wise course. Much effort is wasted and much remains undone when precise plans do not guide the analysis.

Another theme of this chapter is the analyst's interaction

with the decision maker. The decision maker is the beginning and the end of the CBA cycle. Initially, the decision maker must communicate to the analyst a detailed description of the problem to be addressed and the nature of the information desired, such as, the scope of the sensitivity analysis or the emphasis of the social impact analysis. The analyst's design of the CBA will reflect, in large measure, the requirements of the decision maker. The completed CBA is finally used by the decision maker as an aid in making the requisite decision. The CBA is an information-processing "machine." The decision maker's input to the analyst will affect the analyst's output to the decision maker. The better the problem is specified, the more useful will be the final report to the decision maker.

A schematic representation of the major steps in CBA is presented in Figure 9.1. Some of the steps have already been discussed in detail; the others are the primary subject matter of this chapter. The numbers adjacent to each block refer to that the chapter section dealing with that topic.

9.2   DEFINING THE PROBLEM

Although defining the problem to be analyzed may appear to be an almost trivial task, any CBA veteran will testify otherwise. This first step gives direction to the remainder of the analysis. It is here that the decision maker plays a crucial role, communicating to the analyst precisely what he wishes to be done. It is the analyst's task to record these desires, and elicit whatever information is needed to exactly define the problem. While each project has its own unique features, many aspects of problem definition are common to most, and, although such a listing can never be complete, it forms a basic checklist for *both* the analyst and decision maker. A discussion of these aspects is given below.

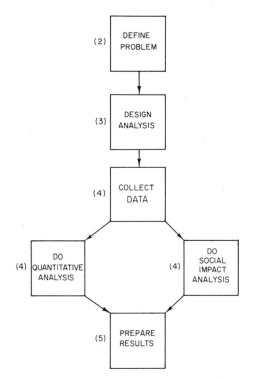

Figure 9.1 Flow diagram depicting major steps in performing a cost-benefit analysis (numbers in parentheses refer to section in text dealing with the corresponding step).

9.2.1 Project Scenario

A technical description and a detailed scenario definition for the projects to be analyzed are obviously important initial steps. The main point here is that explicit recognition should be given to all resource inputs and final outputs of the projects, and the calendar time in which they will occur. On the input side, these descriptions must include the types and amounts of resources (for example, numbers of scientists, managers, clerical staff;

various types of capital components for initiation, operation, and maintenance of the projects; and amount and nature of land needed to site the facilities). On the output side, the time streams of each final good of the projects (for example, electrical energy, miles of highway, and retrained manpower) are equally important. The nature and physical dimensions of "externalities" (for example, smoke, noise, and water pollutants) must also be communicated to the analyst.

Often, some of this information will not be available. This lack of information is not detrimental to the analysis as long as this lack is recognized and dealt with, not ignored. The usual ways of solving this information problem are either to perform a simultaneous "engineering" study to determine unknown technical values or to parameterize the unknown values in recognition that the final results will be *conditional* on the assumed parameter values.

9.2.2   Baseline Scenario

Similarly, a technical description and detailed scenario of the universal alternative—the status quo—should be constructed. Every project has an alternative, even if it is to "do nothing," for to "do nothing" implies a time stream of costs and benefits to society just as a positive project does. Of course, it is exactly this "do-nothing" or baseline scenario with which each project is compared. The CBA focuses on how a project will change the baseline time stream of social well-being. Thus, only the *differences* between the baseline time stream and the *with-project* time stream are considered in CBA. The "good" differences are the benefits of the project; the "bad" differences are the costs. Since the *difference* that the project will make is of primal importance, it is essential to have the baseline scenario with which to compare the project scenario. An example will clarify this need for a baseline scenario.

Consider a project to provide electric energy by using wind, that is, "windmill" construction. Suppose that the social cost of a windmill—the value of the resources used to build a windmill—is known. Are the benefits the value of the electricity produced? Not necessarily. It depends on the baseline scenario. If, in the absence of windmills, conventional means of producing electricity would be expanded so that members of society would get the same amount of electric energy without as they would with windmills, the benefits would be in the value of fuel saved by conventional power generators, not in the extra electricity. There would be no *difference* in electricity generated, but there would be a *difference* in the amount of oil, for example, that could be put to alternative uses by society. On the other hand, if the baseline scenario provided less electricity than did the windmill project, at least part of the benefits of the project would be in the value of electricity produced by windmills.

9.2.3 Definition of Society

Cost-benefit analysis is an attempt to assess social costs and social benefits; that is, CBA takes the public point of view. As the reader will recall from Chapter 4, the value of a project is the sum of its value to each member of society. Clearly, then, costs and benefits depend on who is included in society. For projects at the national level, the usual definition is that society consists of all United States citizens. At the regional, state, and local levels, the operational definition of society is not so easily posited for there are often benefit and cost spillovers (externalities) beyond the stipulated geographical bounds of the project. For example, a state-level manpower-training program has obvious spillover benefits: some persons who receive training will eventually migrate out of that state. Benefits will accrue to both residents and nonresidents of the state. Which benefits are to be counted in the CBA? The most appealing *normative* answer (to economists) is that *all* benefits ought to be counted. However, there are any number of circumstances in which this will not be very palatable. If the training program were financed entirely by taxes on state residents, political realities might dictate that the benefits to the residents outweigh the costs, irrespective of whoever else gains. The point here is that the decision maker must define the "society" that the analyst is to examine. Almost inevitably, some uncounted effects will occur and spill over onto persons not included in the society of the CBA. When this spillover is apparent, the analyst should point it out to the decision maker. To reiterate, the decision maker is the final authority on the bounds of "society" for the purposes of the CBA.

9.2.4   Constraints on the Project

It may be necessary that, to be chosen, a project must satisfy a number of diverse constraints. Such constraints may be budgetary, legal, social, political, or institutional. These, of course, must be communicated to the analyst at the start of the CBA. This early communication will enable the analyst to quickly exclude alternative projects that obviously are not feasible. It is impossible to completely explore the scope of each type of constraint; however, an example of each will convey their spirit:

Budgetary
> The initial cost of the project cannot exceed $X and annual operating costs cannot exceed $Y.

Legal
> Pollution caused by the project cannot exceed some set standards.

Social
> Benefits and costs of the project cannot be divided along racial lines.

Political
> Benefits and costs of the project cannot be inequitably divided among different political jurisdictions, for example, states.

Institutional

The project cannot usurp the powers of Institution X in favor of Institution Y, for example, place matters pertaining to the Department of Agriculture in the domain of the Atomic Energy Commission.

Although the placement of a particular constraint in a particular category may be somewhat arbitrary, the important point is that each constraint be explicitly recognized to the extent possible and incorporated into the analysis. It is the decision maker's task to inform the analyst of all such constraints.

9.2.5 Direction of Social Impact Analysis

One can argue that, in principle, the analyst should have free rein over the social impact analysis. After all, he must carefully describe all relevant nonquantifiable effects of the projects in an objective manner. However, the harsh realities of time and budgetary restrictions often impede a completely thorough approach. Thus, when the analyst is forced to trade off one area of investigation against another, it is useful to be aware of the decision maker's preferences and needs.

Accepting the decision maker's direction in the social impact analysis should not undermine the integrity of the analyst's report. The previous paragraph may cause alarm in those who feel that the decision maker often has biases and his influence will alter the neutrality of the CBA. Although the existence of bias is, of course, a possibility, the analyst must flatly state in his report which areas have not been investigated, and also state his opinion as to whether such an investigation would affect the overall assessment of a project. In addition, he should state to what extent the choice of areas for social impact investigation was influenced by the decision maker. In this way, the decision maker may be accommodated without a sacrifice of CBA integrity.

9.2.6   Control Variables

Often, all the technical details of a project will not be initially specified by the decision maker. Rather, the analyst will be charged with choosing optimal values for some variables, such as scale, location, start-up time, or number of installations. These can be termed *control variables*. In a strict sense, optimization falls outside the domain of CBA and generally into the domain of optimization methods.

The variables to be optimized, if any, should be clearly distinguished from those to be parameterized. Ordinarily, the latter are outside the control of the decision maker (sometimes called "state variables") and the former are not. However, the distinction is not always so clear-cut, and the decision maker and analyst should agree on which nonspecified variables are to be optimized and which merely are to be parametrized.

9.2.7   Discount Rate

As mentioned previously, the discount rate is best considered a policy variable, to be set by the decision maker. He may desire that a single rate be used, or he may request that several values be considered. Alternatively, he may wish critical values to be computed. The analyst must get this direction from the decision maker.

9.2.8   Time Horizon

The time horizon is also a policy variable, although it is not as volatile an issue as the discount rate. The decision maker must decide how far into the future that costs and benefits are to be projected and thus counted into the net present value of the project. Ordinarily, most costs of a public project are incurred in its early years, and so a truncated time horizon has the effect of excluding more benefits than costs from consideration. Thus, a time horizon places a conservative bias on the NPV calculation, but it should be realized that with time horizons of 50 years or more, the bias is very slight. The discounting process is such that values occurring 50 years or more in the future add little to present value. Clearly, the higher the discount rate chosen, the shorter is the time horizon that should be considered.

9.2.9 Data Sources

Although source identification and data gathering are responsibilities of the analyst, it will often be the case that the decision maker, through his or her own investigations prior to commissioning the CBA, will have come across relevant data sources. The analyst, in the interest of saving time, should explore such possibilities before initiating his own searches.

9.2.10 Format of Results

Throughout these discussions, it has been stressed that the analyst's task is to present the decision maker with all the relevant information in a convenient format. Although this may not seem to be an important point, the convenience of the format may well affect the extent to which the decision maker utilizes the CBA as a decision aid. Thus, the analyst should elicit from the decision maker his preferences regarding the scope of the sensitivity analysis, use of critical values, and what general level of "technical language" should be used in the report proper.

9.2.11 Summary

In summary, *defining the problem* is the first step in a CBA and it requires close cooperation and communication between the decision maker and analyst. Insofar as it gives direction to the rest of the study, defining the problem should be treated as a major part of a CBA. Failure to invest time in problem definition almost invariably results in confusion and wasted efforts in the remainder of the study.

9.3   DESIGNING THE ANALYSIS

The formal design of the cost–benefit analysis should be done during its early stages, before plunging into data collection and cost and benefit estimation. The six basic points involved in carrying out the design are discussed below.

9.3.1   The Problem Structure

Determining the analytic structure of the problem follows directly from defining the problem. The purpose here is to determine which *measure* (for example, net present value or benefit–cost ratio) to employ in comparing alternatives. In Section 2.3, the relation between the structure of a problem and the decision measure to employ was discussed. The main aspects of structure are the dependence or independence of projects, the type of constraints, and the variables to be optimized. At this stage of the design, the analytic structure of the problem should be written out as carefully as possible, and all vagaries should be uncovered.

9.3.2   Preliminary Identification of Costs and Benefits

The identification problem was discussed at length in Chapter 3. Basically, there are two ways of discovering costs and benefits: searching for affected goods and services or searching for affected persons. In practice, it is useful to employ both of these approaches, remembering, however, that *each is a different way of arriving at the same costs and benefits*. That is, either the commodities or the persons approach is a good way to discover effects, but only one can be used to count a cost or benefit. Using both results in double counting. How are the affected commodities and persons to be discovered? A number of complementary ways can be used to suggest what interrelationships exist between the project and the rest of the economy:

(a) economic theory.
(b) Professional literature dealing with previous similar projects.
(c) The scenarios developed in defining the problem.
(d) Introspection.
(e) Brainstorming with colleagues.
(f) Interviews with interested persons, including the decision maker.

Thus, the result of this step is a list of costs and benefits that are likely to be incurred with each project under consideration.

9.3.3 Assessment of the Listed Costs and Benefits

This assessment is with respect to validity and quantifiability. With regard to the former, the analyst must be wary of including transfer payments or sunk costs as social benefits or costs. He must also be sure that true values are not being double counted. It then must be determined whether, to what extent, and in what dimensions each valid cost or benefit can be quantified. This determination requires a cursory survey both of data availability and of the potential of gathering new data.

9.3.4 Scope and Dimensions of the Quantitative Analysis

In principle, a CBA should deal with *all* the costs and benefits of a project. Some of these will be quantified; the others will be treated in a qualitative fashion. It is not too great a departure from conventional usage to bring all of the qualitative analysis under the umbrella term of "social impact analysis." Of necessity, some costs and benefits such as intangibles can be treated only qualitatively. Among the quantifiable costs and benefits, some may not be quantified in the CBA because of time and budgetary restrictions. Of those that are quantified, some will be specified in money terms and others will be accorded their own dimensions (incommensurables). However, by no means is there a well-defined boundary between incommensurables and the costs and benefits that have ready dollar values. It is probably best to consider the costs and benefits of a project as lying along a spectrum of "quantifiability," ranging from intangibles through incommensurables to market goods. Intangibles would include the effects of the project on such things as social justice, social harmony, personal freedom, democracy, or aesthetics. These all involve values beyond the economic and do not exhibit even likely dimensions for measurement, much less actual numerical values. Incommensurables would include lives lost, injuries and illnesses sustained, national defense, other public goods such as recreation facilities, and some externalities. Evidently, incommensurables may involve economic or noneconomic values. Their distinguishing characteristic is that they may be readily quantified, but not in money terms. For example, measurements can easily be made of number of lives lost, number of work days lost owing to illness, or number of user days of a recreation facility. Measurements can even be made of national defense as a *probability* of forestalling preemptive nuclear attacks, or as a *percentage* of population surviving after an enemy's first strike. Of course, to a greater or lesser extent, these measurements are not easily converted into dollar values.

Market goods are agricultural products, textiles, electricity, automobile servicing, and the like—any good or service exchanged through a market. The most important feature of a market good is the existence of a corresponding market price that, subject to the qualifications outlined in Chapter 4, is a direct measure of social value in money terms.

Thus, with regard to a spectrum of "quantifiability," all

nonquantifiable costs and benefits fall into the intangibles range, and all quantifiable effects are in the incommensurable or market-goods range. Only effects in the market-goods range, however, are readily measured in money terms. There is no clear-cut boundary between any of the ranges in the spectrum, and it often happens that some cost or benefit will appear to lie somewhere between incommensurables and market goods. Such a cost will be readily measurable in nonmonetary terms but will also appear to be convertible into a meaningful dollar value. As an example, such costs may be associated with recreation benefits, or losses resulting from illnesses or injuries. One of the major problems faced by the analyst is determining how far to go in converting apparent incommensurables into dollar values. Some observers would argue that the analyst should convert all effects into dollar values, even intangibles. The idea is simply that the NPV thus computed captures everything. This complete conversion virtually obviates the role of the decision maker, since he could easily be replaced by a 3 × 5 file card containing such immutable rules as: If NPV > 0, accept the project. This notion—total conversion into dollar values—has probably been the greatest source of criticism of CBA. Fortunately, the advocates of that notion seem to be waning in strength.

On the other hand, a CBA that fails to convert very many effects into dollars will not be a successful decision aid, for the decision maker then will be forced to compare projects on the basis of two- or three-dozen dimensions, a situation not too far removed from "eyeballing" raw data. Once again, then, how far is the analyst to go in converting seeming incommensurables into dollar values? Although there is no categorical answer, the decision maker can specify to the analyst those apparent incommensurables for which he can accept dollar conversions and those for which he cannot. The decision maker and the analyst can jointly determine the dimensionality of the results. In effect, with the technical aid of the analyst in elucidating relevant trade-offs, the decision maker determines the cutoff point in the cost-benefit spectrum between effects usefully measured in dollars and those better measured in their own dimensions. This process would appear to be the only way the analyst can ensure that his approach to quantification will be acceptable to the decision maker in the sense that the results are credible and thus useful as a decision aid.

In brief, this discussion has centered on determining the scope and dimensionality of the quantitative part of the CBA. Implicitly, then, the breadth of the social impact analysis (the qualitative part of the CBA) is determined simultaneously, for whatever effects are not quantitatively analyzed must be qualitatively analyzed, at least cursorily. The factors affecting this determination are given in Figure 9.2. There is no denying that

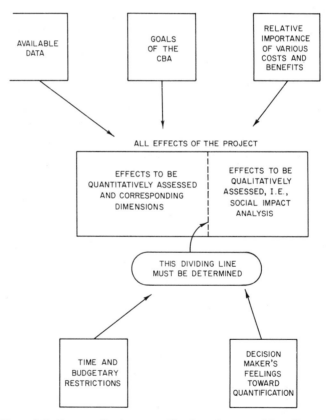

Figure 9.2   Factors affecting quantification of costs and benefits.

the analyst must exercise his own judgment in allowing each of these factors to influence his determination.

9.3.5 Choice of Sensitivity Analysis

The three broad levels of sensitivity analysis discussed in Chapter 8 were subjective, partial, and general. There it was pointed out that the choice of which level of sensitivity analysis to employ depends on the inevitable trade-off between time and resources spent on one part of the CBA and time and resources spent on another, and how this relates to the quality of the overall CBA. It was also mentioned that, under certain circumstances, mean values alone are sufficient to guide the decision maker, obviating the need for extensive sensitivity analysis. Finally, the desires of the decision maker must be considered. There is no point in developing extensive probability distributions of net present value if the decision maker will not use the information. Of course, the analyst should perform that analysis when the decision maker expresses the desire for such information. Once again, this issue must be decided by the good judgement of the analyst.

9.3.6 Determination of Data to Be Collected

This flows directly from the discussions in Sections 9.3.4 and 9.3.5. Once the nature of the quantitative analysis is set and the type of sensitivity analysis that will be employed is known, the necessary data to accomplish these tasks is manifest. Essentially, the process described in Section 9.3.4 determines the category of data needed (for example, price of electricity in 1985) and that described in Section 9.3.5 determines whether point estimates are needed, or whether bounding estimates should be used, such as high and low values in addition to a medium "best" estimate, or whether corresponding probabilities of occurrence need be sought.

9.4   COLLECTING THE DATA

Although it is not necessary to go into a detailed discussion on collecting data, a few common sense considerations deserve mention. *Planning* the format of the collected data is extremely important. The format should specify the number of significant figures for each entry, should allow easy access to any part of the data, and should be capable of quick updating. The data should be gathered from original sources when possible. By using original sources one minimizes the risk of recording errors which creep into transcribed data. All of the qualifications to the data should be accurately recorded. Finally, the sources of all data should be recorded for eventual reference in preparing the footnotes and bibliography.

9.5   PERFORMING THE ANALYSIS

Quantitative analysis was treated at length in Chapters 4–6. The essence of this task is the use of raw data and the economic theory of Chapter 4 to make good estimates of social costs and benefits. The identification of such costs and benefits was discussed in Chapter 3. If a thorough job of designing the analysis (discussed above) has been done, the analyst hopefully will encounter no major problems at this stage. Performing a thorough job is not to say that every estimate will be precise, only that any lack of precision will be acknowledged either verbally or in formal sensitivity analysis. The quantitative analysis includes finding "best" point estimates of the social value of a project along with a sensitivity analysis.

Performing the social impact analysis, defined to include an examination of noneconomic effects, was discussed in Chapter 7. In this part of the analysis, all nonquantified effects are brought out as clearly as possible. As mentioned previously, some aspects may receive more extensive treatment at the expense of other aspects. There is no objection to this type of treatment as long as the relative importance of each effect is not obscured, and the analyst holds fast to a completely scientific (that is, neutral) viewpoint.

9.6 PRESENTING THE RESULTS

Throughout this book, three key points emerge time and again:

(1) CBA depends on the proper identification and measurement of all project effects.

(2) Incommensurables and intangibles, which are those effects that are not susceptible to quantification or monetization, must be acknowledged and displayed as accurately as possible.

(3) CBA, ultimately, is an aid to the decision maker.

These three points provide, in a sense, the critical test of a CBA accounting scheme. Such a scheme must permit the comprehensive itemization of project effects and their corresponding quantification, along with the qualitative assessment of intangibles, all in a format useful to the decision maker.

A CBA accounting scheme should also lend itself to the special demands that are often made on project analyses. These special demands include analyses of project impacts on regional development, income redistribution among income classes, the environment, and social values in general.

An accounting format designed to fulfill the foregoing requirements is presented in Figure 9.3. All project effects with which the analyst has associated dollar values are listed under *monetized effects*. Here, the entries are generally descriptive. However, quantitative information can also be presented, as when the particular effect is an "incommensurable." For both

| | | BENEFITS (NPV) | | | | | | | COSTS (NPV) | | | | | | |
| | | NATIONAL | REGIONAL | | | INCOME CLASS | | | NATIONAL | REGIONAL | | | INCOME CLASS | | |
	PROJECT EFFECT	I + II + III -L + M + U	I	II	III	L	M	U	PROJECT EFFECT	I + II + III -L + M + V	I	II	III	L	M	U
MONETIZED EFFECTS — REAL FINAL GOODS AND SERVICES																
1	SUM REAL BENEFIT								1 SUM REAL COSTS							
2	TRANSFERS								2 TRANSFERS							
3	REGIONAL ACCOUNT								3 REGIONAL ACCOUNT							
4	INCOME DISTRIBUTION								4 INCOME DISTRIBUTION							
NON-MONETIZED EFFECTS — ENVIRONMENTAL	AESTHETICS								AESTHETICS							
	IMPORTANT SITES								IMPORTANT SITES							
	WATER AND AIR QUALITY								WATER AND AIR QUALITY							
	IRREVERSIBLE CONSEQUENCES								IRREVERSIBLE CONSEQUENCES							
	OTHER								OTHER							
SOCIAL	LIFE								LIFE							
	HEALTH								HEALTH							
	SAFETY								SAFETY							
	EDUCATION								EDUCATION							
	CULTURE								CULTURE							
	RECREATION								RECREATION							
	EMERGENCY PREP.								EMERGENCY PREP.							
	OTHER								OTHER							

NOTE: LINE 3 - LINE I + LINE 2
LINE 4 - LINE I + LINE 2

Figure 9.3 CBA accounting work sheet.

benefits and costs, the national entries are analyzed into regional and income-class components. Line 1 is a summary of the real direct effects of the project. Line 2 allows whatever income transfers are present to be displayed. Line 3 is a summary of the monetary effects on a regional basis; Line 4 is a summary of the effects by income class.

Obviously, this one-page format is more suggestive than practical. Few cost–benefit analyses can be summarized so easily. For a complex project, each block could contain numerous entries; for a simple project, most blocks could be blank. In any case, and whatever the scheme adopted, the point is that a summary must be produced which is clear, succinct, complete, and understandable. A cost–benefit analysis is useful only when it is accessible.

BIBLIOGRAPHY

Arrow, K. J., and R. C. Lind, Uncertainty and the evaluation of public investment decisions, *American Economic Review* **50** (1970), 364-378.

Bator, F. M., The anatomy of market failure, *Quarterly Journal of Economics* **72** (1958), 351-379.

Baumol, W. J., On the social rate of discount, *American Economic Review* **58** (1968), 788-802.

Buchanan, J. M., and G. Tullock, *The Calculus of Consent*. Ann Arbor: Univ. of Michigan Press, 1962.

Coase, R. H., The Problems of Social Cost, *Journal of Law and Economics* **3** (1960), 1-44.

Currie, J. M., J. A. Murphy, and A. Schmitz, The concept of economic surplus and its use in economic analysis, *Economic Journal* **81** (1971), 741-799.

Dasgupta, A. K., and D. W. Pearce, *Cost-Benefit Analysis*. New York: Barnes and Noble, 1972.

Dasgupta, P., S. Marglin, and A. Sen, *Guidelines for Project Evaluation*. New York: United Nations, 1972.

Davis, O. A., and A. B. Whinston, Externality, welfare and the theory of games, *Journal of Political Economy* **70** (1962), 241-262.

Dorfman, R., ed., *Measuring Benefits of Government Investments*. Washington, D.C.: Brookings Inst., 1965.

Dupuit, J., On the measurement of utility of public works, *International Economic Papers* **2** (1952), 83-110 (translated from French, 1844).

Eckstein, O., Investment criteria for economic development and the theory of intertemporal welfare economics, *Quarterly Journal of Economics* **71** (1957), 56-85.

Eckstein, O., *Water Resources Development: The Economics of Project Evaluation*. Cambridge, Massachusetts: Harvard Univ. Press, 1958.

Feldstein, M. S., Net social benefit calculation and the public investment decision, *Oxford Economic Papers* **16** (1964), 114-131.

Friedman, M., The Marshallian demand curve, *Journal of Political Economy* **57** (1949), 463-495.

Friedman, M., and L. J. Savage, Utility analysis of choices involving risks, *Journal of Political Economy* **56** (1948), 279-304.

Gittinger, J. P., *Economic Analysis of Agricultural Projects*. Baltimore, Maryland: Johns Hopkins Univ. Press, 1972.

Griliches, Z., Research costs and social returns: Hybrid corn and related innovations, *Journal of Political Economy* **66** (1958), 419-431.

Henderson, A. M., Consumer's surplus and the compensating variation, *Review of Economic Studies* **8** (1941), 117-121.

Hicks, J. R., The foundations of welfare economics, *Economic Journal*, **49** (1939), 696-712.

Hicks, J. R., The four consumers' surpluses, *Review of Economic Studies*, **11** (1941), 31-41.

Hicks, J. R., *A Revision of Demand Theory*. Oxford: Clarendon Press, 1956.

Hirshleifer, J., J. C. DeHaven, and J. W. Milliman, *Water Supply: Economics, Technology, and Policy*. Chicago: Univ. of Chicago Press, 1960.

Hitch, C. J., and R. N. McKean, *Economics of Defense in the Nuclear Age*. Cambridge, Massachusetts: Harvard Univ. Press, 1960.

Hotelling, H., The general welfare in relation to problems of taxation and of railway and utility rates, *Econometrica* **6** (1938), 242-269.

Kaldor, N., Welfare propositions of economics and interpersonal comparisons of utility, *Economic Journal* **49** (1939), 549-552.

Krutilla, J. V., and O. Eckstein, *Multiple Purpose River Development*. Baltimore, Maryland: Johns Hopkins Univ. Press, 1958.

Little, I. M. D., *A Critique of Welfare Economics*, 2nd ed. London and New York: Oxford Univ. Press, 1957.

Little, I. M. D., and J. A. Mirrlees, *Project Appraisal and Planning for Developing Countries*. New York: Basic Books, 1974.

Maass, A., Benefit-cost analysis: Its relevance to public investment decisions, *Quarterly Journal of Economics* **80** (May 1966), 208-226.

Maass, A., et al., *Design of Water Resource Systems: New Techniques for Relating Economic Objectives, Engineering Analysis and Government Planning*. Cambridge, Massachusetts: Harvard Univ. Press, 1962.

Marglin, S. A., The social rate of discount and the optimal rate of investment, *Quarterly Journal of Economics* **77** (1963a), 95-111.

Marglin, S. A., The opportunity costs of public investment, *Quarterly Journal of Economics* **77** (1963b), 274-289.

Margolis, J., The economic evaluation of federal water resource development, *American Economic Review* **49** (1959), 96-111.

McKean, R. N., *Efficiency in Government through Systems Analysis*. New York: Wiley, 1958.

Merewitz, L., and S. H. Sosnick, *The Budget's New Clothes*. Chicago: Markham, 1971.

Mishan, E. J., The relationship between joint products, collective goods, and external effects, *Journal of Political Economy* **77** (1969a), 329-348.

Mishan, E. J., *Welfare Economics: An Assessment*. Amsterdam: North-Holland Publ., 1969b.

Mishan, E. J., *Cost-Benefit Analysis*, New expanded ed. New York: Praeger, 1976.

Nash, C., D. Pearce, and J. Stanley, An evaluation of cost-benefit analysis criteria, *Scottish Journal of Political Economy* **22** (June 1975), 121-133.

"National Environmental Policy Act of 1969," *U.S. Statutes at Large*, 91st Congress, 1st Session, Volume **83,** 852-856.

Pearce, D., The limits of cost-benefit analysis as a guide to environmental policy, *Kyklos* **29** (1976), 97-112.

Pigou, A. C., *Economics of Welfare*, 4th ed. New York: Macmillan, 1946.

Prest, A. R., and R. Turvey, Cost-benefit analysis: A survey, *Economic Journal* **75** (1965), 683-735.

Rothenberg, J., *The Measurement of Social Welfare*. Englewood Cliffs, New Jersey: Prentice-Hall, 1961.

Samuelson, P. A., The pure theory of public expenditure, *Review of Economics and Statistics* **36** (1954), 387-389.

Samuelson, P. A., *Foundations of Economic Analysis*, 2nd ed. Cambridge, Massachusetts: Harvard Univ. Press, 1963.

Samuelson, P. A., *Economics*, 9th ed. New York: McGraw-Hill, 1973.

Schumpeter, J. A. *History of Economic Analysis*. London and New York: Oxford Univ. Press, 1954.

Scitovsky, T., A note on welfare propositions in economics, *Review of Economic Studies* **9** (1941), 77-88.

Scitovsky, T., Two concepts of external economies, *Journal of Political Economy* **67** (1954), 143-151.

Steiner, P. O., Choosing among alternative public investments in the water resource field, *American Economic Review* **49** (1959), 893-916.

The Holy Bible. King James Version. London: Cambridge University (no date).

Turvey, R., On divergences between social cost and private cost, *Economica* **30** (1963), 309-313.

U.S. Bureau of the Budget. Reports and budget estimates relating to federal programs and projects for conservation, development, and use of water and related land resources, Circular A-47, Washington D.C., 1952.

U.S. Federal Interagency River Basin Committee, Subcommittee on Benefits and Costs. *Proposed Practices for Economic Analysis of River Basin Projects*. Washington D.C.: U.S. Government Printing Office, 1950.

U.S. Office of Management and Budget. Discount rates to be used in evaluating time-distributed costs and benefits, Circular A-94 (revised), Washington D.C., March 27, 1972.

U.S. Water Resources Council. *Policies, Standards and Criteria for Formulation, Evaluation and Review of Plans for Use and Development of Water and Related Land Resources*, Senate Document 97, 87th Congress. Washington, D.C.: U.S. Government Printing Office, 1962.

U.S. Water Resources Council. Principles, standards, and procedures for water and related land resource planning, *Federal Register* **38**-174 (Sept. 10, 1973), Part III.

INDEX